# TABLE OF CONTENTS

## PARISHES IN THE HOLBEACH UNION

Fleet, Gedney, Gedney Hill, Holbeach (inc. Holbeach Drove, Holbeach St John), Sutton Bridge, Sutton St Edmund, Sutton St James, Sutton St Mary (or Long Sutton), Sutton St Nicholas (or Lutton), Tydd St Mary, Whaplode and Whaplode Drove.

# INTRODUCTION

All references to paupers from the minute books of the meetings of the Board of Guardians for Holbeach Union Workhouse from October 1868 to September 1880 are included in this book. The Lincolnshire Archives reference to the appropriate Minute Book will be found at the top of each page.

In 1865 the Union became the place of settlement rather than the parish, one years residence without receiving relief giving settlement in a particular Union, and this is reflected in the entries found in these minutes. Paupers are still being removed from one Union to another; relatives of paupers are being pursued for payment towards their maintenance; boys are being apprenticed to the sea at Grimsby; non-resident paupers and non-settled paupers are regularly mentioned.

## THE WORKHOUSE SYSTEM

In 1834 the **Poor Law Amendment Act** was passed. By this act a number of parishes were grouped together into a **Poor Law Union**. It may have been necessary for the Union to use several small existing workhouses until a larger workhouse was built.

The **Poor Law Commissioners** administered the new workhouse system and it will be seen in these minutes that they were often applied to for advice in the early years. Individual workhouses were administered by a **Board of Guardians**. One or more **Guardians** were appointed to represent each parish within the Union, and the Board of Guardians, with an elected Chairman, met each week or fortnightly, to discuss any issues to do with the running of the workhouse including specific pauper cases. The **Relieving Officer** was the person to whom any pauper living within the Union should apply for relief. The pauper could be given "out relief" in cases of illness, or an "order for the House" in any other case. The **Overseers of the Poor** continued the work they had done in their own parishes before the act was passed. **Medical Officers** were appointed and were given a specific group of parishes, the pauper inhabitants of which they were required to visit if circumstances required. **Medical certificates** were given to paupers needing out relief. Other officers appointed by the Board of Guardians were the **Master** and **Mistress** or **Matron** of the Workhouse. These were often a husband and wife. The Master took his directions from the Board of Guardians, and was in day to day control of the Workhouse. Under the Master were the **Schoolmaster** and **Schoolmistress**, and the **Porter**. Finally, and perhaps the most important officer was the **Clerk to the Guardians**, who wrote the wonderful material that has survived to this day and which gives us a valuable insight into the plight of the paupers and the day to day running of the workhouse.

When a pauper applied for relief, several questions would be asked. Most importantly, where was his place of settlement? Had he any relatives who could pay his maintenance? Had he any income from other sources that would maintain him and his family through difficult times? Was the father of a bastard child able to support him? All these questions are posed in the minute books, and often satisfactorily answered. It is important to remember that any pauper had to apply to the Relieving Officer of the Union in which he resided. If his settlement turned out to be within a different Poor Law Union he could be removed to the Union in which his place of settlement was supposed to be. If no appeal was made against the removal order within 21 days, his place of settlement was proven, and once proved, where the pauper was relieved was irrelevant as his maintenance, either in or out of the workhouse, was paid by the Union to which he belonged. There would, therefore, be many paupers living within a particular Union whose places of settlement were in a different Union.

# EXTRACTS FROM THE HOLBEACH UNION WORKHOUSE MINUTES
## PL8/102/18 1868 - 1871

5 October 1868. **Biggadike** Inquest. Unanimously resolved that the Clerk write to M$^r$ E **Woods** one of the juryman who sat upon Biggadike's inquests asking him whether the Rev$^d$ J. F. **Francklin** either at the inquest or prior thereto made private statements to him and others of the jury prejudicial to the Board and endeavour to induce the jury to bring in a verdict against the Relieving Officer **Coxon** or in default thereof to bring in a verdict of Censure against the Guardians respecting Biggakike's death. [Page 1]

19 October 1868. **Biggadike** John. Mr E **Woods** in reply to the Boards letter of last week stated that prior to the inquest I had no conversation whatever on the subject with the Rev$^d$ John Fairfax **Francklin** – At the inquest he the Rev$^d$ John Fairfax Francklin expressed his opinion privately to him as also to another Juryman that strong censure ought to be voted against the Relieving Officer (**Coxon**) or in default thereof against the Board of Guardians.

The above communication having been read in the presence of Mr Francklin and the Chairman having asked whether Mr Francklin had any statement to make in explanation M$^r$ Francklin thereon said I shall not talk to a man like you (meaning the Chairman) I shall go for my solicitor – and forthwith left the Boardroom.

Proposed by M$^r$ Vice Chairman **Blower** That the conduct of the Rev$^d$ John Fairfax Francklin at the Inquest on the body of John Biggadike on which occasion he it is stated upon the evidence of several competent witnesses to have called the Guardians scamps and rascals and who ought to be hung for manslaughter is too contemptable for further notice. Seconded by M$^r$ David **Carbutt** and unanimously carried.

A letter from M$^r$ Alfred **Clarke** M$^r$ Francklins Solicitor was read asking to be present at the discussion with reference to Mr Francklins conduct.

Resolved that M$^r$ Clarke be informed that the discussion with reference to M$^r$ Francklins alleged conduct touching Biggadikes matter is at an end.

Resolved that all letters and enquiries upon this matter pass through the Board. [Page 2]

19 October 1868. **Boulding** Widow. A letter from the Nottingham Union was read stating that W$^m$ Boulding was dead and the widow was badly off. Ordered that she be allowed 3/6 per week and 4lb bread. [Page 2]

19 October 1868. **Slator** Rebecca. The Chairman stated to the Board that the Clerk to the Guardians and the Relieving Officer of the Basford Union had been to see him on the subject of the prosecution and they offered to share in the expenses and it appeared that the womans statement could not be thoroughly relied upon. Resolved that the matter be settled on the terms of each Union paying their own expenses. [Page 2]

19 October 1868. Resolved that a pauper named **Thickpenny** have two days leave of absence to seek work. [Page 3]

2 November 1868. A letter dated 21 October 1868 from the Poor Law Board was read sanctioning the payment of the sum of £3 in the case of Frank **Whiley** to M$^r$ A. B. **Ewen**. [Page 4]

2 November 18668. A letter dated 19$^{th}$ October 1868 from the Poor Law Board was read sanctioning the payment of the sum of £2 to M$^r$ Henry **Ewen** in the case of James **Munson**. [Page 4]

2 November 1868. A letter from the Rev$^d$ J. F. **Francklin** to the Board with reference to **Biggadikes** case was read. A letter from the Rev$^d$ J. F. Francklin to the Chairman was read. No discussion took place upon the two preceding letters. [Page 4]

2 November 1868. Overcrowded house at Holbeach. It having been brought to the notice of the Board that the house in which John **Pearman** resided in Holbeach was too small for the family and that some of them were suffering from diarrhoea Resolved that the Officer of Health for Holbeach have notice thereof. [Page 5]

2 November 1868. It having been mentioned at the Board that Ann **Warren** was not so frequently attended by the Medical Officer (of the Gedney Hill District) as her case required Ordered that M$^r$ **Sturkey** be written to calling his attention to the case. [Page 5]

16 November 1868. Non resident Poor. The attention of the board having been called to the amount of relief administered by the Boston Guardians to Mary **Cook** a pauper chargeable to this Union Ordered that the Clerk write to the Boston Board asking them the cause of the increased relief. [Page 6]

16 November 1868. **Betts** Ann. Ordered that Relieving Officer **Winfrey** procure a warrant for the apprehension of Ann Betts for deserting her four children viz Elizabeth aged 11 years Louisa 9 years James 6 years and Hannah 3 years. [Page 6]

16 November 1868. **Wellfare** Jane applied to the board for relief for herself and three children stating that her husband had deserted her and that he went by the name of **May**. Ordered that Relieving Officer **Coxon** procure a warrant for the apprehension of Thomas Wellfare otherwise Thomas May for deserting his family. Ordered that the settlement of the above paupers be enquired into. [Page 7]

14 December 1868. A letter from the Kings Lynn Union dated 28th ult. asking whether this Board had any objections to Walter **Byron** being apprenticed to Mr Kelham **Hoyte**. Mr Hoyte having informed the Clerk that he had no intention of taking an apprentice from the Union. It is resolved that the Clerk report accordingly. [Page 9]

28 December 1868. Lunacy. An order from the County Asylum was read discharging Edmund **Bailey** from the County Asylum. Ordered that application be made to the father of the above named Edmund Bailey for the balance of maintenance due from him to the 21 Decr. [Page 11]

28 December 1868. **Burgess** Emily. Relieving Officer **Winfrey** reported that Emily Burgess had been conveyed to the County Asylum and that her settlement was not in this Union. Resolved that the settlement be enquired into. [Page 11]

28 December 1868. **Pearman** and family. Ordered that the Clerk enquire into this paupers settlement. [Page 11]

25 January 1868. **Baxter** Catharine aged 15 years. William **Shortland** of Whaplode Marsh having agreed to take this inmate into his service and allow her 30/- per annum It is resolved that she be provided with clothing to the amount of 30/-. [Page 17]

25 January 1868. Lunatics. A notice from the County Asylum was read announcing the death of Mary **Dixon** aged 85 years and who was recently sent to the Asylum. [Page 17]

8 February 1868. Lunacy. A certificate dated 28 January 1869 under the hands and seals of two of the Visiting Justices was read discharging Matilda **Parrot** from the County Asylum. Relieving Officer **Winfrey** reported that a pauper lunatic had been discharged from the said asylum but no certificate was produced (Sarah **Eason**). [Page 19]

8 March 1869. **Hood**. Mr Edward **Holland** of Whaplode having appeared before the Board with Edward Hood aged 15 years and late an inmate of the workhouse and the Boy having been examined apart from his proposed master and in the presence of his said proposed master they both appeared satisfied. Unanimously resolved that Hood be bound for a period of 5 years and that a premium of £10 be given to be paid in the usual manner and the said Edward Holland agrees to find him pocket money at the rate of 3d per week for the first two years 4d per week for the following two years and 6d per week during the last year. [Page 25]

8 March 1869. **Jackson** Sarah. Mr Kelham **Hoyte** having applied through the Master of the workhouse for permission to take Sarah Jackson aged 14 years on trial for a month as domestic servant. Resolved that Sarah Jackson be allowed to go to Mr Hoytes and that the master make terms as to wages and if approved clothing to the value of 50/- be allowed. [Page 25]

15 March 1869. Apprentices. Mr **Porter** of Grimsby appeared before the Guardians with reference to the two boys Wm **Mabletoft** and Alfred **Young** and the Boys having assented to go to Sea It is Resolved that the premium be £10 each and that they be bound for five years. Mr Porter being desirous of taking the two boys with him it is Resolved that he be allowed 20/- towards the expenses. [Page 27]

15 March 1869. Mary **Hudson** of Gosberton having applied to the Master to have her sister out of the workhouse for the purpose of obtain a situation for her and the Board having been satisfied that the sister would properly provide for the child – Ellen **Booth** – It was resolved that Ellen Booth be provided with clothing to the value of £1-15-0. [Page 27]

22 March 1869. The Indenture apprenticing Edwd **Hood** was signed by the Master and the Apprentice and the Seal of the Board attached to the Indenture by the Chairman. [Page 32]

22 March 1869. **Grummitt** Jane. Settlement Langtoft in the Bourn Union residence Whaplode. A letter from the Bourn Union dated 19 March was read asking this Board to relieve with 3/- and 4lb bread weekly. Ordered that Relieving Officer **Coxon** relieve as requested. [Page 32]

5 April 1869. Lunatics. A notice dated 25th March 1869 was read signed by the Visiting Justices discharging John **Balls** from the County Asylum. [Page 38]

5 April 1869. **Reed** George having deserted his wife and family and being at work upon the Midland Line of Railway between Peterborough and Wesbech It is ordered that he be apprehended. [Page 38]

19 April 1869. A letter dated 9th April 1869 from the Poor Law Board sanctioning the payment of the sum of £10 to Lucy **Simpson**. [*Miss Simpson was the cook*] [Page 43]

19 April 1869. Lunacy. The authorities of the Lincoln County Asylum informed the Guardians that Abigal **Palmer** died on the 10th instant. [Page 43]

19 April 1869. M[r] **Jex** Plumber applies to have Amos **Bennett** apprenticed to him the Boys father has deserted him and his mother is dead (aged 14). Resolved that Mr Jex be allowed to take the boy for trial during a period of one month. [Page 43]

3 May 1869. Ordered that the Poor Law Board be asked to approve the payment of 30/- towards the clothing of William **Barnes** the son of Joseph Barnes an ablebodied laborer – and that the Poor Law Board be informed the youth is about to be apprenticed to (M[r] **Lemon**) a watch maker that he is afflicted with continuous bleeding at the navel in a way that defies Medical Assistance. [Page 46]

3 May 1869. **Hoyte** Kelham appeared before the Board and agreed to take Sarah **Jackson** wages 30/- per year and clothing 30/- an agreement to be signed. M[r] Hoyte afterwards refused to take the girl in consequence of the stipulation being introduced into the agreement viz wages to be paid quarterly. [Page 46]

3 May 1869. Ordered that the Clerk report to the Thrapston Union that W[m.] **Neville** relieved by this Union on behalf of that Union died during the 4th week of the present quarter. [Page 47]

17 May 1869. Resolved that M[r] **Leaper** be asked whether he had apprehended **Read** for desertion of his family. The Guardians were informed that the man was at work between Thorney and Peterborough. [Page 49]

17 May 1869. Resolved that Dr **Harper** be requested to report to the Board at their next meeting on the case of David **Eason** a pauper inmate. [Page 49]

31 May 1869. The Clerk reported that Jane **Creek** a pauper Lunatic chargeable to this Union died in the County Asylum on the 18th instant. [Page 51]

31 May 1869. **Betts** Jemima. The Spalding Union having written asking the Guardians to receive this pauper without orders of removal and the case being fully inquired into the Guardians are satisfied she could be removed under orders of removal. Resolved the pauper be admitted into the Workhouse and that the Master have notice to receive her and enter her name in the Whaplode list. [Page 51]

31 May 1869. **Nidd** Emma and six children. The Guardians of the Braintree Union (by letter dated 27th May) applies to have these paupers received without orders of removal stating that Nidd gained a settlement in Long Sutton by apprenticeship with M[r] W[m] **Fletcher**. The Board being of opinion that Nidd gained a settlement elsewhere the Clerk is ordered to inform the Guardians of the Braintree Union that the family cannot be received without orders of removal. [Page 51]

31 May 1869. George **Kingston** absconding in the workhouse clothes to be apprehended. [Page 51]

31 May 1869. **Creek** Mary Jane a pauper Lunatic in the Lincoln County Asylum. A certificate from the County Asylum was produced showing this pauper died on the 18 May inst. [Page 51]

31 May 1869. **Hall** a pauper in the service of M[r] **Parkinson** of Gedney Drove End applied for out relief in consequence of an accident he had whilst in the service of his Master an agreement was produced showing Hall to be a yearly servant. Ordered that M[r] Parkinson be informed that he is bound to maintain his servant that he be asked to repay the relief this day given. [Page 51]

31 May 1869. **Elwood** Elizabeth. Her settlement to be investigated – lives at M[r] **Anderson**s. [Page 51]

14 June 1869. **Betts** Jemima. A letter from the Spalding Union was read stating that the pauper could not be removed and that the relief would be charged in the non settled poor account. [Page 53]

14 June 1869. County Police (Negligence of). The Master reported that warrants had been obtained and issued to the police for the apprehension of John **Finn** George **Kingston** and [*blank*] **Reed** and information given as to where they were last seen but no apprehension had taken place.

Unanimously resolved that the Chief Constables attention be drawn to these facts and that he be requested to institute enquiry thereon. [Page 53]

14 June 1869. **Smart** Amos. A letter from the Hailsham Union was read stating that Amos Smart was in the County Asylum at Howards Heath and that he belonged to this Union and asking this Board to take him without orders of removal also that the sum of £28.8.5 was due for maintenance and removal to the Asylum. Ordered that the Clerk of the Hailsham Union be informed that in the opinion of the Board the Lunatic is not chargeable to this Union. [Page 53]

28 June 1869. **Burgess** Emily a Lunatic. The Clerk reported that an order dated 17th June had been received from the County Asylum ordering this person to be removed from the asylum in consequence of her having so far recovered that it was expedient she should be out in trust. [Page 56]

28 June 1869. **Wilson** Harriet. Ely Union. A letter from the Ely Union discontinuing the relief to this pauper and her family was read. Ordered that insomuch as this pauper cannot maintain herself and children that the Guardians be asked to send an order for their admission into the Ely Workhouse. [Page 56]

26 July 1869. An order under the hands and seals of two Justices of the Peace for the County of Surrey was read ordering the payment of care maintenance of Richard Arton **Palmer** in Peckham Asylum the said order alleging him to belong the parish of Holbeach in this Union. Order that depositions be applied for and the settlement searched into. [Page 61]

26 July 1869. R. O. **Winfrey** reported that Bridget **Cartwright** had been sent to the County Asylum on the 23rd instant. [Page 61]

26 July 1869. **Cooley** Susanna. It being reported to the Guardians that the husband of this pauper was at work at the Kings Cross Railway Station it is resolved that he be summoned to show cause why he neglects to maintain her. [Page 61]

26 July 1869. **Coopers** relief. R. O. **Coxon** the Inspector of Nuisances having reported that the house of Mr **Victory** (the father in law of the pauper) was too small to be occupied by three grown up persons. It is resolved that the relief be discontinued. [Page 61]

26 July 1869. **Bugg** Ann. Ordered that the Guardians of the Spalding Union be asked to relieve Ann Bugg (Whaplode) aged 71 years and who resides with her son in law James **Watts** with 3/- commencing from the 12th instant. [Page 61]

9 August 1869. **Palmer** Richard Arton a lunatic in Peckham House Asylum. A copy of the depositions have been applied for and from which it appeared that Edward Nicholas **Rolfe** of Camberwell had sworn that Palmer had not obtained any other settlement than a birth settlement. It is ordered that Robert **Millns** proceed and make enquiries as to the truth of the depositions. [Page 63]

9 August 1869. **Slator** John. It being reported to this Board that John Slator was living in an immoral state – Ordered that he be requested to attend before this Board at the next meeting for the purpose of making just arrangements for the maintenance of his wife in the Lincoln County Asylum. [Page 64]

9 August 1869. **Creek** late a lunatic. Mrs Creek through Mr **Proctor** applied for her daughters clothing the daughter having died in the County Asylum. Ordered that the clothing be given up. [Page 64]

9 August 1869. **Furnage** [blank]. Ordered that the husband of this lunatic be advertized for and that £1-1-0 be offered for his apprehension and that a warrant be obtained. [Page 64]

9 August 1869. **Clarke** Jemima the wife of Wm Clarke appeared before the Board and stated that her husband neglected to maintain her and her children. Relief was ordered and RO **Coxon** is requested to take out a summons against William Clarke. [Page 64]

9 August 1869. **Finch** Martha. A letter dated this day from the Revd Arthur **Brook** was read stating that in the opinion of Dr **Harper** the child would be benefited by sending her to the Margate Hospital and offering a ticket for her admission if the Board would give the amount per week which she costs in the house. Resolved that the offer be accepted and Mr Brook be forthwith informed thereof. [Page 65]

9 August 1869. **Burgess** Emily. An order dated 25 July signed by two justices was read permanently discharging Emily Burgess was read. [Page 65]

9 August 1869. **Taylor** Richard. An order dated 28th July 1869 under the hands and seals of two Justices of the Peace and which order discharges on probation Richard Taylor late a pauper

Lunatic in the Lincoln County Asylum for a period of one month also ordering him 5/- per week during that period. [Page 65]

23 August 1869. **Palmer** Richard Arton. Enquires having been made with reference to the settlement of this Lunatic and it having been ascertained that he had not obtained any other settlement than that of birth – It is ordered that the amount mentioned in the order be paid and that steps be taken for removing him to the Lincoln County Asylum. [Page 66]

23 August 1869. **Slator** Sarah a Lunatic. Since the order made at the last meeting of the Guardians for summoning the husband of this lunatic to appear before the Board a notice has been received of her death consequently the husband did not appear to make fresh arrangements for his wifes maintenance. [Page 66]

23 August 1869. **Gunn** Mary Ann aged 16 years was admitted into the Workhouse. She stated she was born at Coningsby the child was brought to RO **Coxon** by M$^r$ **Fuller** who resides with William **Burrell** in the Barn Yard. Ordered that the father be sought up for the purposes of maintaining her also that the Medical Officer be asked whether the case is one of permanent disability. [Page 66]

6 September 1869. **Warrener** Robert. The Clerk reported that on examining the Masters books – That Robert Warrener aged 12 years had been admitted in consequence of having met with an accident and that the father of the boy was foreman to Mr T. **Worth** – the Master of the house explained to the Board that the Boy was sent to the infirmary by D$^r$ **Harper**. Unanimously resolved that D$^r$ Harper be requested to inform the Board by next Board day his reasons for sending Robert **Warner** to the workhouse when he was not a pauper and his friends were in a position to maintain him. [Page 69]

6 September 1869. **Gunn** Mary. M$^{rs}$ **Fuller** (the person who brought this pauper to the Union at the last Meeting of the Guardians) applied to the Guardians for leave to take the pauper away stating she had obtained a place of service for her. Resolved that M$^{rs}$ Fuller be allowed to take the child away. [Page 69]

6 September 1869. Ordered that R. A. **Palmer** be removed from Peckham Asylum Surrey to the County Asylum. [Page 70]

20 September 1869. **Warrener** Robert. Ordered that application be made to this man for the maintenance of his son now an inmate of the Infirmary. [Page 72]

20 September 1869. **Taylor** a Lunatic. An Order from the County Asylum dated 16$^{th}$ Sept$^r$ 1869 was read permanently discharging Richard Taylor from the Asylum. [Page 73]

18 October 1869. Lunatics. Richard Arton **Palmer** a pauper belonging to this Union died on the 16 instant at Camberwell. [Page 84]

1 November 1869. **Finch** Martha. A letter from the Superintendent of the Royal National Hospital for Scrofula Margate was produced stating that if a further sum of 24/- was sent she could stay 4 weeks longer. Resolved that the amount required be sent. [Page 85]

15 November 1869. Holbeach Common. M$^r$ **Harper** reported that a nuisance complained of by him had not been attended to he also complained that his suggestion to the Relieving Officer had not been carried out with reference to the supply of mutton to a poor person named **Fenn**. M$^r$ Harper being present and one of the Inspectors of Nuisances for the parish of Holbeach also being present he denied that any nuisance existed and on M$^r$ Harper being asked where the nuisance was he stated he was not the Inspector neither did he know where the nuisance was but though Fever could not exist with some cause.

M$^r$ Harper verbally stated that the house of **Papworth** was overcrowded in consequence of one of his rooms being filled with gleant corn.

Relieving Officer **Coxon** was requested to see the house and take steps for removing the corn out of the house also to supply disinfecting fluid where necessary and other dsinfect$^s$. [Page 88]

28 November 1869. Fever on the Bank. R O **Coxon** reported he had visited the house of the pauper **Papworth** on the Little Common but he had not caused the wheat to be removed as requested. Ordered that Mr Coxon see that the corn is forthwith removed. [Page 90]

29 November 1869. **Finch** Martha. Resolved that this relief be continued for another month and that a cheque be sent for the amount. [Page 91]

29 November 1869. Resolved that a summons be obtained against Richard **Mumby** (residing at M$^r$ W$^m$ **Naylor**s Cowfield Gould farm in Holbeach) for not maintaining his wife. [Page 91]

13 December 1869. The Relieving Officer for the Long Sutton District reported he had not taken proceedings against **Mumby** in consequence of having been repaid a part of the relief advanced. [Page 93]

13 December 1869. Dr **Harper** reported to the Guardians that R O **Coxon** was highly sensurable in the case of Jane **Pickett** in refusing relief.
Coxon appeared before the Board and stated that Jane Pickett and her husband lived with her father and stepmother in part of the Staffs house – that he Coxon had offered to pay the step mother for nursing her step daughter anything she required. That he Coxon had observed that they had a good fire; that the father and husband were both capable of going to work and that he Coxon had refused to give the man anything for himself.
John Pickett the husband appeared before the Board and stated he was in full work but had to stay at home to nurse his wife they have two bedrooms Pickett and his wife also their three children sleep in one room and **Westmorland** and his wife in the other room.
D^r Harper was present at the examination. The Guardians are of opinion that Coxon had relieved liberally and dealt fairly with the case. [Page 93]

13 December 1869. **Whiley** Thomas. The Guardians of the Kingston Union having sent orders to this Union for the removal of Thomas Whiley whom it is alleged was born in this workhouse and who had not resided in the Kingston Union one year neither was his relief rendered necessary by sickness or accident.
Ordered that M^r Richard **Blundy** late brewer at Long Sutton be written to asking him to enquire into the settlement of Thomas Whiley. [Page 93]

23 December 1869. The Clerk was requested to sign the punishment book approving of 9 strokes to **Bennett** and 10 to **Baxter**. [Page 94]

23 December 1869. **Jackson** W^m. Ordered that W^m Jackson be apprehended for deserting his children. [Page 94]

27 December 1869. **Finch** Martha. Notice having been received from the Margate Royal Sea bathing Infirmary to remove Martha Finch. Resolved that the Matron fetch her home. [Page 96]

27 December 1869. **Rigall** John Apprenticed to Mr J. W. **Jackson** Plumber Long Sutton. A letter was received from the apprentice complaining of ill treatment, bad living the past nine months not having sufficient to eat that he gets no fresh meat it is always old bones stewed and old kept meat three or four days together and that he could not eat it the pies are made of bad meat black potatoes there has been maggots in the meat for breakfast and tea they have stinking fat and bread - to drink his tea out of basins – that his master sent him to M^r **Wright** of Lutton and M^rs Wright saw he was ill and gave him food and when his master arrived at M^r Wrights he scolded the boy and said he should "not stuff my guts as the Guardians did".
The apprentice appeared before the Board and was requested to make any further complaint he might have. He then stated I sleep in the attic in the roof the bed is 3 feet wide for two of us to sleep in the room is about 8 feet high on one side and slopes to the floor it is about 7 feet wide and 8 feet long the window is about one foot wide and 15 or 16 inches long I light fires, wash floors and have washed dishes, I empty at times the chamber utensil used by me and the other apprentice, and make our bed – my master strikes me that is pushes me about George **Skeef** the other apprentice being present confirmed the above statement.
Resolved that Rigall go to Dr **Harper** to be examined. [Page 96]

27 December 1869. **Riggal** & **Jackson**. Dr **Harper** came to the Union and wrote the following certificate
"I have examined John Rigall I do not find any evidence of corporal punishment nor do I find evidence of the boy being badly fed I _fear_ he has mischief begining in the apex of the lungs on the left side and in such cases I should recommend that the boy be warmly clothed and not unnecessarily exposed to inclement wether.
Dec^r 27^th 1869                          Robert Harper
Unanimously resolved that the Clerk prosecute Jackson forthwith. [Page 97]

10 January 1870. **Rigall** John. Ordered that an advertizement be issued for a carpenter or wheelwright place. [Page 100]

10 January 1870. **Wilson** James & Wife. This man having an income of £20 per annum and having been admitted into the workhouse And the Rev^d Arthur **Brook** having induced Wilson to sign a

paper assigning his pension to the Guardians but which paper was useless the Relieving Officer was requested to get the proper Loan Book signed at once when it appeared **Coxall** had left it with a shopkeeper at Gedney Hill for him to obtain a signature thereto. [Page 100]

10 January 1870. James **Perkins** aged 18 years March 19th last is desirous of being bound apprentice to William **Wain** of Fleet shoemaker and Mr Wain having agreed to take him until he is 21 years of age. It is resolved that the premium be £12, the first moiety to consist of Clothing to the amount of £3 and cash £3 and the remaining moiety at the expiration of one year from the date of binding. Mr Wain to pay the youth 6[d] weekly as wages – and in consequence of Perkins being a cripple and in case of constitutional illness the Guardians will find Medical attendance and necessaries. [Page 100]

10 January 1870. **Holland**s family – Luton Union. A letter from the Luton Union was read confirming the payment of 2/- each to Hollands orphans. [Page 101]

10 January 1870. Ordered that the Indentures for binding Alfred **Youngs** and William **Mabletoft** be prepared & that £10 each be paid by the Guardians to Mr William **Porter** (the Master of the apprentices), by two equal instalments. [Page 101]

10 January 1870. Resolved that the Poor Law Board be written to asking them to sanction the admission of two children into the workhouse under the following circumstances viz.
John **Gent** aged 40 years – a widower residing at Lutton having seven children aged 10, 8, 6, 5, 4 & 2 years and one 9 months – his earnings being twelve shillings weekly and 20 stones bacon yearly which is not sufficient to maintain his numerous family. [Page 101]

24 January 1870. A letter from the Spalding Union was read asking this Board to confirm the payment of 25/- for clothing to John **Samson** a pauper residing in the Spalding Union but chargeable to this Union. Resolved that the same be allowed. [Page 102]

24 January 1870. **Gent**s two children. A letter dated 22nd January 1870 from the Poor Law Board was read refusing to sanction the admission of Gents two children into the workhouse and stating as a reason it would be relief in aid of wages. [Page 102]

24 January 1870. Extra Medical fee. A letter dated 21st January 1870 from the Poor Law Board was read sanctioning the payment of twenty one shillings to M[r] A B **Vise** in David **Atkinson**s case of Hydrocele. [Page 102]

24 January 1870. **Nidd** Emma. An order of removal was received from the Braintree Union for removing Emma Nidd aged 43 Richard aged 15 Russell aged 13 John aged 11 Robert aged 8 Mary aged 6 and Edwin aged 4 years residing at Bocking in the Braintree Union to the parish of Gedney Seadyke in this Union. Unanimously resolved that the settlement be sought into and the order appealed against as defective there being no such parish as Gedney Seadyke in this Union. [Page 102]

24 January 1870. Spalding Union. Thomas **Murfitt** has come to live with his daughter Mrs **Sussam** applied for relief, his settlement is Spalding he requires 3/- weekly. [Page 103]

24 January 1870. The Seal of the Board was affixed to the Indenture binding James **Perkins** apprentice to William **Wain** of Fleet & signed by the Master and apprentice. [Page 103]

24 January 1870. The Indentures for binding Alfred **Youngs** and William **Mabletoft** apprentices to William **Porter** was produced. Resolved that the Indentures be sent to Grimsby for execution and that the same be returned to have the Seal of the Board affixed. [Page 103]

7 February 1870. Braintree Union. There being an error in the orders of removal there being no such parish in this Union as is described in the order it is ordered that the Clerk take opinion of Counsel as to opposing the order. [Page 104]

7 February 1870. Stimulants. Mr. **Wood** complained of the manner in which M[r] **Bellairs** butcher of Gedney Hill gave out the gin. Mr **Crowder** had recommended that a pint of gin should be given to the wife of Joseph **Hinton**. Mr Wood produced a bottle in which the gin was put up and on measuring the quantity it held it would appear that M[r] Bellairs had given about a quarter of a pint instead of a pint. Ordered that the matter be enquired into at the next meeting of the Board. [Page 104]

7 February 1870. M[r] **Roper**s relief. The Clerk having pointed out to the Guardians that this paupers relief was paid only quarterly instead of weekly and this being contrary to the order of the Poor Law Board and consequently an illegal payment. Resolved that the payments be continued quarterly as heretofore through M[r] **Knott**. [Page 105]

21 February 1870. Ordered that M$^r$ Robert **Brett** of Long Sutton be applied to to maintain his son William Brett. [Page 107]

21 February 1870. It is also ordered that the Seal of the Board be affixed to the Indentures binding William **Mabletoft** and Alfred **Youngs** apprentices to Mr **Porter** smack owner Great Grimsby. [Page 108]

7 March 1870. Lambeth to Gedney. An order of removal from the parish of Lambeth was read stating that Shadrack **Rising** gained a settlement by residing with a M$^r$ **Bell** in Gedney – that about 53 years ago he was hired as a yearly servant at wages by the said M$^r$ Bell that he resided with his said master one whole year that he constantly resided and slept in the house of the said M$^r$ Bell. It was resolved that no further steps be taken in the matter. [Page 110]

7 March 1870. A letter from the Spalding Union was read stating that the Guardians of that Union were surprised by having an application from a M$^{rs}$ **Robinson** of Fleet on behalf of her aged father J **Beach** and stating that R. O. **Coxon** had refused to give relief other than Medical relief and referred M$^{rs}$ Robinson to the Spalding Union.
Ordered that the Guardians of the Spalding Union be informed that M$^{rs}$ Robinson has misstated the case of Beach and that at a former meeting of this Board the Guardians thoroughly investigated the case and after due consideration offered the pauper such relief as they deemed expedient the man does not reside in Coxons District neither did Coxon see the woman. [Page 111]

7 March 1870. **Nidd** family. A letter from M$^r$ A **Cunnington** of Braintree was read asking the Guardians to relieve M$^{rs}$ Nidd and family at Braintree where she was partially employed and that he would undertake to pay her on behalf of this Union. Resolved that M$^r$ Cunnington be informed that the Guardians are quite willing to relieve but the relief must be paid by the Guardians of the Braintree Union through their officer and that M$^{rs}$ Nidd had better apply to that Union. [Page 111]

7 March 1870. That M$^r$ A B **Ewen** be written to enquiring whether it is necessary to see Clement **Meatheringham** oftener than once in 9 days it appearing from M$^r$ Ewens report that he had not seen him for that period. [Page 113]

7 March 1870. Sarah **Scott** an ablebodied woman the wife of formerly an inhabitant of Sutton Saint Edmunds but now of Sutterton appeared before the Board. She had become chargeable to this Union in consequence of her husband refusing to maintain her. It is ordered that the Clerk obtain a summons against the husband to show cause why he neglects to maintain his wife. [Page 113]

21 March 1870. **Nidd** and family. The Clerk of the Braintree Union having written stating that M$^r$ **Cunnington** would pay any relief this Board thought necessary but the Guardians of the Braintree Union declined to open any non settled poor accounts. Proposed by M$^r$ **Sunderland** that the Clerk of the Braintree Union be informed that this Board will repay any relief advanced by M$^r$ Cunnington Mrs Nidd might require if the RO of that Union would investigate the case and report what she will require. Seconded by M$^r$ **Fletcher**. Carried Unanimously. [Page 115]

21 March 1870. A letter from Ann **Coulson** of Wisbech was read applying for payment for the maintenance of Edward **Gosling** a pauper who broke his leg whilst in a helpless state of intoxication she also stated the pauper informed her the Guardians would pay. Ordered that M$^{rs}$ Coulson that Gosling had no authority for stating the Guardians would pay and that her application is refused. [Page 115]

28 March 1870. Ordered that the Poor Law Board be written to asking them to sanction the sum of £3 to M$^r$ A B **Ewen** for performing operation of Paracentesis Abdom$^s$ twice in the case of Ruth **Edens**. [Page 117]

28 March 1870. M$^r$ **Crowden** having charged the sum of £1.0.0 in the case of Sarah **Mackman** in consequence of inflamation in the womb after confinement
Visits and Medicine
Resolved that M$^r$ Crowden be informed that no such fee is allowed by the order of the Poor Law Board and that the sum charged be struck out until further enquiry is made as to the number of visits and the length of times these visits extended over. [Page 117]

4 April 1870. **Crowden** James S. Having charged £1.10.0 for extra services in the case of Sarah **Mackman**. Resolved that Mr Crowden having been paid 10/6 in this case the Guardians would not be justified in paying a further sum of £1-10-0. [Page 121]

4 April 1870. Apprentice. Edward **Holland** brought his apprentice Edward **Hood** before the Guardians and the youth having been questioned in the absence of his master as to his treatment

and the replies being satisfactory It is resolved that Edward Holland be paid the balance of premium. [Page 122]

4 April 1870. Ordered that Elizabeth **Ouzman** be removed to her place of settlement. [Page 122]

4 April 1870. Ordered that Frances **Lister** and her five children be removed to Liverpool. [Page 122]

18 April 1870. A letter from the Poor Law Board – N° 146743 dated 8 April 1870 was read approving of the payment of £3 to M$^r$ Arthur Benjamin **Ewen** in the case of Ruth **Edens**. [Page 125]

18 April 1870. **Peck** Henry a Lunatic. John **Young** the brother in law applies to have this Lunatic from the private Asylum at Lincoln to the County Asylum. Peck has four children without means of maintaining themselves. M$^r$ Young agrees to pay half the cost of maintenance in the asylum. Resolved that D$^r$ **Palmer** the Medical Superintendent be requested to obtain an order for the removal of Henry Peck from the Lincoln Asylum to the County Asylum and charge the cost of maintenance to this Union. [Page 125]

2 May 1870. **Lister**s family. A letter from the Poor Law Board dated 22 April 1870 with reference to paying the expenses of William Listers family to Liverpool stating that it was contrary to the established rule to sanction the payment of expenses for the purpose of assisting emigration of poor persons to any other than a British Colony, or of women who are deserted by their husband. Resolved that the Poor Law Board be written to again stating the woman is deserted and impress upon them the desirability of their consenting in this instance to depart from their usual course. [Page 127]

2 May 1870. **Wright** Mary Ann settlement Holbeach aged 47 years and two children viz George aged 14 years and Elizabeth aged 12 years – these paupers are residing at Moulton Eugate. Resolved that the Guardians of the Spalding Union be requested to relieve the above named paupers with 2/- and 8lbs bread weekly. [Page 128]

2 May 1870. **Ford.** Ordered that the Clerk write for a truss 20½ in. right side. [Page 128]

16 May 1870. **Holland** George of Whaplode bricklayer applied to have Amos **Bennett** an orphan aged 15 years (who was admitted into the workhouse from Holbeach) bound apprentice to him and the youth having been upon trial appeared before the Board and stated he was satisfied with the place. It was resolved that Bennett be bound apprentice to Holland for a period of four years – that the premium be £10 and payable pursuant to the consolidated orders and Holland agrees to pay the boy two pence per week for the first year 4$^d$ per week during the second year and sixpence per week during the remaining two years – That the usual Indenture be prepared. [Page 129]

16 May 1870. **Dolton** Fanny – whose settlement is in Holbeach – she has been residing with her aunt in Spalding and has 2/- weekly from this Board. The Aunt (and child) appeared before the Guardians stating she had procured a situation for the pauper and was not in a position to find clothing. Resolved that the Clerk write to the Spalding Union requesting them to advance 15/- worth of clothing and discontinue the former relief. [Page 129]

30 May 1870. The master reported that William **Nicholls**, Henry **Constance**, James **Wilson**, George **Parr** & Henry **Green** had absconded from the workhouse with the clothing belonging to the Guardians. Resolved that inasmuch as Nicholls has deserted as many as eleven times and having this time disposed of the jacket belonging to the Union that he be prosecuted and a place obtained for him on one of the training ships. Resolved that the Master of the Workhouse do prosecute the remaining boys to be punished as ordered in the workhouse punishment book. [Page 131]

30 May 1870. **Bennett** an apprentice. George **Holland** appeared before the Board with Amos Bennett the Indenture were duly signed and cheque ordered to be drawn and signed for the premium and clothing – the period of binding for 4 years. [Page 131]

30 May 1870. M$^{rs}$ **Lee** the wife of Moses Lee appeared before the Board and stated her brother Sam$^l$ **Marshall** was apprenticed by the Guardians to M$^r$ **Walker** bricklayer Whaplode – that her brother had not been paid the weekly allowance expressed by the Indenture that the master knocks the boy about – that he is continually swearing at him – that the boy blows the bellows of the church organ on a Sunday and that his master takes nearly all the money for it that he has not sufficient bed clothing – and the boy informs his sister that through his ill treatment he shall have to run away. Resolved that R O **Coxon** examine the Boy and get the M. O. to examine into the state of health of boy and report whether in his opinion he is properly fed. [Page 132]

13 June 1870. **Marshall** an apprentice the Guardians having investigated the charges brought by his sister against **Walker** but from the information given by the Medical Officer **Vise** and the R. O. there does not appear any ground for the complaint. [Page 134]

13 June 1870. Ordered that W^m **Manton** be apprehended for deserting his children and leaving them chargeable to the Holbeach Union. [Page 136]

27 June 1870. **Barnes** a Wandering Lunatic. R. O. **Winfrey** produced a letter sent by William **Chappe** constable of Wisbech which letter stated that Barnes was well known to him and that some months since we sent him to Fulham Asylum & that a month ago (May 26) a letter was sent to M^r **Jude** RO announcing his escape – and on the 19^th inst he was apprehended by the police who reported the fact to the R. O. who informed him they could do nothing with him if absent from the Asylum over 14 days consequently he was discharged. The Lunatic having wandered to Long Sutton Sergt. **Crawford** took him into custody and he [*sic*] It is ordered that he be sent to the Union Workhouse until enquiries can be made. [Page 136]

27 June 1870. The Master reported he had caused William **Manton** to be apprehended and appeared before the Justices and that the Justices adjourned the hearing of the case until the 29^th July provided that Manton did not make any arrangements with the Guardians. [Page 137]

27 June 1870. **Usher** – Gedney Hill District. A remark appears on the Medical Report for the Gedney Hill District – that M^r **Boor** the Overseer of the Poor for the parish of Whaplode and that Mr Boor had revoked such order – that the M. O. had attended on the Thursday Friday and Saturday and it was stated at the Board that on Monday Mr **Redhead** went to Mr **Crowden** to visit M^r Redheads mother in law (Mrs Usher) and that M^r Crowden could not go until Tuesday. Resolved that M^r Crowden be requested to furnish this Board with any observations he may have to make in this matter. [Page 138]

27 June 1870. **Roof.** Resolved that enquiries be made into the settlement of William Roof who resides in Long Sutton. [Page 138]

11 July 1870. A letter from M^r A. B. **Ewen** with reference to Mary **Knight**s - case of confinement - in which case he had attended 18 times and had charged £2. Resolved that the charge be allowed. [Page 140]

11 July 1870. Mr **Crowden** of Gedney Hill appeared before the Board with reference to the case of [*blank*] **Usher** also with reference to his in Medical fees – he explained the several items therein to the satisfaction of the Board and the same was ordered to be paid together with a further sum of 10/6 in the case of M^r **Mackman**. [Page 140]

11 July 1870. The time for paying the Relief advanced to M^rs **Gunthorpe** by the Rev^d E. A. **Fisher** having elapsed – It is ordered that the Poor Law Board be written to asking them to sanction the payment. [Page 142]

25 July 1870. **Barnes** a lunatic. The Clerk reported that he had written to the Wisbech Union with reference to this case – and had received a reply stating that Board declined to receive the Lunatic and that Mr **Jude** the officer referred to as having neglected to appear when requested by M^r **Sharpe** the Superintendent, states that 10 minutes had not elapsed between Sharpe calling upon him and his appearance at the Police Court when he found the Magistrate had discharged the Lunatic on his promising to leave the Town.
Resolved that the Secretary of State – the Poor Law Board and the Commissioners in Lunacy be written to complaining of the unjust proceeding of discharging a wandering Lunatic.
Resolved that the Depwade Union be asked to take the Lunatic without orders of removal he appearing to belong to that union he having been born at Dickleburgh in that Union. [Page 142]

8 August 1870. **Peck** Henry a Lunatic. D^r **Palmer** the Superintendant of the County Asylum reported that Henry Peck died in the Asylum on the 3^rd day of August 1870. [Page 144]

8 August 1870. Ordered as under viz. That D^r **Harper** report whether in his opinion John **Roony** of Holbeach Hurn is permanently disabled.
That D^r Harper report specially upon the case of John **Greathead** as to his bodily health. [Page 144]

22 August 1870. Lunacy. – D^r **Palmer** the Supt. reported that May Ann **Gall** had been discharged from the Lincoln County Asylum. [Page 146]

22 August 1870. An application was made by the Guardians of the Nott^m Union for an order for the admission of Frances **Boulding** into this Workhouse. Ordered that the Clerk send an order to the

Notting^m Union for her admission and that the Master of this Workhouse be instructed to receive the pauper. [Page 146]

19 September 1870. Absconding School Boys. – The Master produced a letter dated the 6^th September instant from the chief Constables office Lincoln stating the two boys Henry **Couston** and W^m **Nicholls** were then in custody of the police, the master had written stating he would submit the letter to the Guardians at their next meeting.
Resolved that the police be forthwith written to and in case they are so in custody that the boys be sent for. [Page 152]

19 September 1870. William **Manton** appeared before the Guardians to ask them to forego the expenses incurred in prosecuting him for leaving his family chargeable to the Union.
The Guardians decline to withdraw the case inasmuch as they can see no extenuating circumstances which would justify them in so doing. [Page 152]

19 September 1870. It was Resolved to admit John **Lawson**s wife into the Workhouse on Lawson agreeing to pay two shillings weekly – Lawson being in the employ of Mr **Boor** one of the Guardians for Whaplode and being present promised to retain 2/- of his wages weekly so long as he continued in his employ. [Page 152]

3 October 1870. Lunacy **Hipkin**. R. O. **Winfrey** reported that Ellen Hipkin had been discharged from the County Asylum. [Page 155]

3 October 1870. **Meek** Robert. A letter from the Lynn Union was read asking to be reimbursed 11/2 the amount paid for a coffin for a poor boy sent from Central Wingland to the Lynn and Norfolk Hospital. Ordered that the amount be paid and included in their next non settled poor account. [Page 155]

3 October 1870. Peterborough Union – non settled poor. The Guardians of that Union having written asking this Board to relieve Ann **French** and her 3 children with 4/6 weekly for a month and afterwards this Board to deal with the case for them – future residence with her father at Long Sutton. Ordered that the relief be paid. [Page 155]

3 October 1870. Wisbech Union. The Guardians of the Wisbech Union having asked this Board to take Harriet **Garton** aged 28 years and her two children Grace Elizabeth aged 3 years and Clarissa aged 5 months alleging the settlement to be in Fleet that he was born in the parish of Fleet in 1836 and who died at Leaham Harbour in May last he was the son of W^m Garton who was born at Long Sutton in 1812 that Harriet Garton was married to the pauper Harriet Garton (formerly **Cotton**) at the parish church at Walksoken in the year 1863.
Resolved that from the evidence produced the paupers inasmuch as there appears to be no settlement in the parish of Fleet. [Page 155]

3 October 1870. Ordered that the Clerk write to the Thrapston Union asking that Board to relieve Martha **Cave** aged 76 years with 3/- weekly and charge the same to this Union. [Page 157]

3 October 1870. Ordered that the Poor Law Board be asked to approve of the payment of the following sums viz.
The sum of £2 to M^r Arthur Benjamin **Ewen** in the case of James **Russell** who was run over by a waggon and sustained a severe wound of the scalp and who has required very long attendance and frequent tedious dressings.
The sum of £1 to Robert **Harper** in the case of infant **Guymer** for Hydrocele.
The further sum of £1 to Robert Harper in the case of Thomas **Goodwin** for Hydrocele. [Page 157]

17 October 1870. Ann **Bowers** a Lunatic. It being reported that this pauper had recovered Ordered that D^r **Palmer** be asked his reasons for detaining her after her recovery. [Page 162]

31 October 1870. **Bowers** a Lunatic. The Clerk reported he had pursuant to the request of the Board written to D^r **Palmer** the Medical Superintendent of the County Asylum and that in reply thereto D^r Palmer stated that Ann Bowers continues irratable abusive and quarrelsome and is subject to frequent paroxysms of manical excitement when she loses all self-control and becomes noisy destructive of clothing filthy in her habits and disgustingly obscene in her language. [Page 164]

31 October 1870. Mr George **Fletcher** applied on behalf of Mr Samuel **Naylor** for the Guardians to admit [blank] **Beckett** a yearly domestic servant into the workhouse. Mr Fletcher stated the servant was ill and unable to do Mr Naylors work. It appeared the girl was still in Mr Naylors service and not destitute consequently this is not a case for the Guardians to deal with. [Page 165]

14 November 1870. **Lewis** Mary aged 23 years the wife of [*blank*] Lewis and James their child aged one year. The Master reported that the husband had deserted his wife and child and that they are now relieved in the workhouse. Ordered that [*blank*] be forthwith apprehended and that the usual reward be offered. [Page 167]

14 November 1870. George **Mabletoft** and Smith **Nicholls** – Mr **Porter** of Grimsby having written that these two boys might be at once sent to him Resolved that in consequence of the Porters sickness and the Master having extra duty to perform that the clerk send some other person with the youths. [Page 167]

28 November 1870. **Parr** a schoolboy. In consequence of this boys conduct being extremely bad for a considerable time past That the Secretary of the "Humber training ship Southampton" 15 Parliament Street Hull be written to by the Clerk enquiring whether Parr can be admitted into that ship. [Page 170]

28 November 1870. Order of Removal for Shadrack **Rising** from the parish of Lambeth to the parish of Gedney in this Union – The Clerk reported he had examined into this settlement under a former order and that the pauper had gained settlement in the parish of Gedney by residing with a Mr **Bell** about 53 years ago. [Page 170]

28 November 1870. **Gardener** Stephen. Jane Gardener the widow of the late Stephen Gardener (who died yesterday) appeared before the Board and stated that her late husband had not been properly treated by the Medical Officer of the Union – that her (SG) was taken ill on Thursday night and was removed to the Infirmary on Friday she stated that the Medical Officer told him he should not be umbug<sup>d</sup> by him. Several witnesses were examined but no evidence was given to show that M<sup>r</sup> **Swann** – D<sup>r</sup> **Harpers** assistant had used any words of the kind referred to M<sup>r</sup> Swann was also present and denied using any unkind words. Proposed by Mr. **Sunderland** and seconded by Mr **Collins** that in the opinion of this Board it is desirable that an inquest be held on the body of the late Stephen Gardener for the purpose of inquiring into the cause of death – so that all parties may be exonerated from blame in the matter. [Page 170]

12 December 1870. **Parr** a schoolboy. A letter from the Secretary of the Training ship Southampton at Hull was read stating that if the boy was sound strong and healthy and if sent under Sec. 14 & 15 of the Industrial School Act 1866 and agree to pay 2/- per week towards his maintenance and if sent to be detained until he attains the age of sixteen years. Resolved that the terms be accepted and that the Clerk take the necessary steps to get Parr admitted into the above named ship. [Page 173]

12 December 1870. **Baxter** a schoolboy being very refractory youth aged 14 years – It is ordered that the Clerk take steps to get him also admitted into the above named training ship. [Page 173]

12 December 1870. **Gardener** Stephen. The Clerk reported that he attended at the Inquest held on the body of the late Stephen Gardener and the following Verdict was returned viz
"Died from disease of heart and that the Jury are satisfied that every care and attention was paid to the deceased by the Medical and other officers of the establishment". [Page 173]

12 December 1870. **Stokes** William aged 9 years now residing in the workhouse admitted from Holbeach. The Medical Officer of the workhouse recommends that this pauper be sent to the Hospital for epilepsy 24 Queens Square London – the Secretary is M<sup>r</sup> **Rawlings**. [Page 173]

28 December 1870. **Stokes** William. A letter from the Hospital for the reception of Epileptic patients was read – but in as much as the parents of the boy had removed him from the workhouse it is deemed advisable to take no further steps in the matter. [Page 176]

28 December 1870. **Winterton** Frances and family. Ordered that the settlement be enquired into and if removable that the Clerk take steps to remove them. [Page 177]

9 January 1871. **Bennett** Amos – Apprentice to **Holland** – Whaplode. The apprentice appeared before the Board and complained that his Master had ill used him. The Guardians investigated the case and found the complaint of ill usage groundless. [Page 181]

23 January 1871. Mr **Barker** appeared before the Board on behalf of Mr John **Carter** brewer of Holbeach for the purpose of enquiring why the officers of the Union declined to admit the Body of James **Feetham** into the workhouse who Mr Barker represented had died in the Street. Mr Barker also stated he wished to be informed as to the Law on the subject. Upon enquiry it appeared the deceased man was taken in a fit as he was about to enter the beerhouse of Mr **Buffham** (the property of Mr John Carter) that he died in such beerhouse and that an inquest was held on the

body on the following morning and that as soon as the coroners certificate was received the Revd **Marshall** enquired of the deceased employers foreman as to the means of burial and then and there gave an order for the decent internment of the deceased. Thereon the Clerk read to the Board the consolidated order applicable to the removal of dead bodies to workhouses and the Board and Cap$^n$ Barker were satisfied that the officers had discharged their duty according to law with perfect regard to decency. [Page 184]

23 January 1871. **Youngs.** W$^m$ Fleet. Ordered that the clerk call M$^r$ **Vises** attention to his report in this case that he has not seen him for three weeks and reports him unable to work the wife states the Doctor has seen them for two weeks last Saturday the woman applied for medicine. [Page 185]

6 February 1871. Lynn Union **Whiley** John. Application being made by the Lynn Union to this Board for 6$^d$ per week additional for this pauper. Ordered that the sixpence additional be granted. [Page 187]

6 February 1871. **Wain** M$^r$ and his apprentice John **Perkins** attended before the Board and applied for the second instalment of (six pounds) the premium. Ordered that the same be paid. [Page 188]

3 April 1871. Apprentices. A letter from the Caistor Union was read stating there was no objection to the binding apprentice of Nicholas **Baxter** and **Mapletoft** to Mr. **Rea** and Mr. **Porter** of Grimsby. [Page 1]

17 April 1871. Non Settled Poor. The Spalding Union having written asking this Board to relieve for them Catherine **Rowthan** or **Rowshan** 74 residing with her sister at Long Sutton with 3/6 weekly – place of settlement not stated – Mary **Franklin** W$^d$ aged 79 settlement Spalding resides with her daughter M$^{rs}$ S. **Tuke** at Lutton with 3/6 weekly. [Page 9]

17 April 1871. Resolved that the indentures binding **Nicholls** apprentice to M$^r$ **Porter** have the seal affixed and signed by the Chairman. [Page 8]

1 May 1871. Ordered that Mr. A **Ewen** be requested to report upon the case of W$^m$ **Watson** residing at Long Sutton. [Page 10]

1 May 1871. M$^r$ W$^m$ **Smith** of Spalding appeared before the Board with reference to the binding apprentice to him of Samuel **Gilbert** a cripple aged 16 years residing at Gedney. Resolved that a premium of £12 be given and 30/- annually in clothing for a term of [*blank*] years. [Page 10]

29 May 1871. A letter from the Freebridge Union was read (27 May 1871) stating that the Guardians of that Union were willing to repay the relief to William **Parks** from this date. [Page 14]

29 May 1871. **Bull** W$^m$. The Guardians of the Leeds Union having submitted a statement to this Union with reference to the pauper named William Bull – and from which statement it appeared that William Bulls settlement is in Whaplode – that he is permanently disabled and is now receiving relief from Leeds – and the Guardians being satisfied that such statement is correct It is ordered that the Clerk do write informing the Leeds Guardians that on W$^m$ Bull being brought to this Union Workhouse he will be admitted. [Page 14]

29 May 1871. Ordered that the Clerk enquire into the settlement of Elizabeth **Taylor** who is now residing with her daughter at Whaplode Drove. [Page 14]

29 May 1871. Ordered that Thomas **Tuplin** be apprehended for deserting his wife and two children. [Page 14]

12 June 1871. Resolved that one guinea reward be given to Police Constable **Crawford** for the apprehension of **Tuplin** who had paid the expenses of his wifes maintenance and the expenses of his apprehension. [Page 16]

12 June 1871. Amos **Bennett** apprenticed to Mr Geo **Holland** appeared before the Board, the Master an apprentice appeared to be getting on satisfactorily – Resolved that a cheque be drawn for the residue of the premium. [Page 18]

26 June 1871. The Visiting Committee reported that Dr **Harper** should be consulted as to the adviseability of sending Rose **Smith** or Hannah **Sweeney** suffering from Rheumatic Gout to the Buxton Hospital. [Page 21]

10 July 1871. Resolved that 30/- be allowed to Harriet **Green** late an inmate of the Union Workhouse and who now resides with Mr Vincent **Eastgate**. [Page 21]

10 July 1871. **Watson** Robert of Gedney Hill applied for the clothing of his late wife who died in the County Asylum. Resolved that he be allowed to take the clothing. [Page 21]

10 July 1871. **Bunn** George Sutton Saint Edmunds aged 47 years. Mr. O **Crowden** suggests that this pauper should have money instead of Brandy. Ordered that the clerk request Mr Crowden the M. O. of the Gedney District state whether the Brandy is really necessary this patient and if the patient needs the stimulant the Guardians are of opinion it had better be supplied as heretofore. [Page 22]

24 July 1871. Devonshire Hospital. Hannah **Sweeney**. Joseph **Taylor** the secretary to this hospital by letter dated the 20 July instant informed the Guardians there would be a vacancy for this pauper on the 13$^{th}$ September next. [Page 24]

7 August 1871. Ordered that thirty five (?) be allowed to **Green** for clothing. [Page 26]

21 August 1871. Maria **Courts**. Ordered that the Clerk write to the Spalding Union asking them to relieve this pauper with 3/6 weekly and charge the same to this Union – Age 76 settlement Holbeach – gone to reside with her son in law John **Smith** sadler Moulton. [Page 29]

21 August 1871. **Gray** David Lutton. This pauper has Medical Necessaries ordered by Medical Officer A B **Ewen** – the name is not entered on the report the man is in a dying state. Ordered that the clerk call Mr Ewens attention to this omission. [Page 29]

4 September 1871. A letter from the Roman Catholic Priest at Wisbech was read applying to be repaid his expenses incurred in attending Timothy **Maxwell** a Member of the Roman Catholic Church

and an inmate of this Workhouse. The Majority of the Guardians present were of opinion the amount ought not to be paid. [*In the margin in purple ink is written* The Rev^d E L **Bennett** & Mr **Blower** – paid 3/- which was transmitted] [Page 32]

18 September 1871. Thomas **May** of Sunderland being desirous of taking his sister (Mary Ann May aged 9 years) out of the Workhouse to reside with him Resolved that May be allowed to take the child if upon enquiry he be found in a position to keep her and that he be allowed 2/- per week for three months and clothings. [Page 39]

2 October 1871. **May** Mary Ann. M^r Nicholas **Neagle** of 10 Lombard Street Sunderland having written stating that Thomas May is married and resides in one of his houses. Resolved that Thomas May be informed that the Guardians cannot pay the expenses of his sister to Sunderland, but they agree to allow him (?)/ per week for thirteen weeks and will also find her some clothing. [Page 41]

2 October 1871. Spalding Union **Patman** Hannah and five children. The Guardians of the Spalding Union having requested this Board to relieve the above named pauper with 7/- weekly. Resolved that the Relieving Officer **Marshall** pay the same on behalf of the Spalding Union. [Page 42]

2 October 1871. **Hood** Catharine. Resolved that 35/- be allowed to this pauper for clothing. [Page 42]

16 October 1871. Albert James **Beckey** (a pauper sent into the house by R O **Winfrey** at the request of the Rev^d E L **Bennett** J.P.) appeared before the Board. He stated he was 7 years of age that his parents died in some Street High Holborn London about 2 years ago that he was born in Whitechapel but did not know in what street. That he had been travelling the country about 2 years he knew no one in London his father had worked at a Foundry but where he did not know. Ordered that the Clerk take immediate steps to remove this child to his settlement. [Page 47]

30 October 1871. John **Chamberlain** an inmate of the Workhouse applied to the Guardians to be apprenticed to M^r **Smith** tailor Crescent Spalding. Ordered that the Clerk write to M^r Smith enquiring whether he had a vacancy for an apprentice. [Page 50] [*See 13 November, page 51, Mr Smith had no vacancy*]

13 November 1871. **Clarke** W^m Medical order. The Clerk having given to pay Medical officer **Harper** to attend Clarke wife during her confinement and the Relieving Officer having stated he declined giving an order not having Clark as he the relieving officer alleged applied to the Medical Gentleman in Holbeach which Clark refused to do but stated he would see Mr **Ayliff** who would make **Marshall** an order or give one himself. Ordered that the propriety of the refusal of Medical relief to William Clark be referred to the Poor Law Board and their opinion taken thereon the Guardians being desirous that the Clerk should not be saddled personally with the cost of the womans labor when attended by R O Harper if the same can be legally disbursed and the circumstances fully stated. All papers relating to the case to be sent to the Poor Law Board. [Page 51]

12 November 1871. **Patman** Hannah Spalding Union. Report to the Spalding Union that in consequence of one child being dead that 1/- weekly be taken off. [Page 52]

12 November 1871. Ordered that Ann **Dack** be removed to her place of settlement. [Page 52]

27 November 1871. **Clarke**s Medical. Ordered that this matter stand over until such time as M^r **Vise** is in condition to make his statement as to Clarks case to the Poor Law Board. [Page 53]

27 November 1871. Ordered that the summons against **Dack** for deserting his children stand over. It was stated he had taken a woman and three children with him to Middlesborough. [Page 53]

27 November 1871. A letter from the Spalding Union was read requesting that the relief to **Patman** and her four children should be discontinued and that on her going to the Workhouse at Spalding she would be admitted (this woman is deserted by her husband). [Page 53]

27 November 1871. On going through the reliefs the Guardians made the following orders:
That John **Howard** his family coming into the house his settlement is to be enquired into.
That Algernon **Ewen** be written to enquiring as to William **Wicks** and his pint of Porter for four years.
Mary **Roberts**. That Mr **Crowden** be written to enquiring into the apparent neglect in this case and that he be requested to report thereon by the next meeting of the Guardians. [Page 54]

11 December 1871. Mr **Crowden** reported that the case of M^rs **Roberts** was that she was worn out and might live for 6 weeks or 6 months that he had examined her carefully for twenty minutes but could detect no symptoms of disease that he gave her medicines for the bowels as requested and

could he have done her any more good, he would have gone daily and do his utmost but it is not in medicine to repair exhausted nature.

Mr. **Boor** and Mr. **Woods** from what they had heard thought the case had been neglected.

Resolved that Mr Crowden be requested to attend personally before the guardians at their next meeting to explain his reason for not giving an earlier attendance to the case of Mary Roberts. [Page 56]

11 December 1871. M$^r$ Thomas **Hales** of Crowland applied to have **Chamberlain** (a youth with only one leg) apprentice to him. It was resolved that he be allowed to take him on trial and should he be found able to stand the business that £14 premium be allowed the Guardians to find Medical attendance in case of sickness and M$^r$ Hales pocket money. [Page 57]

27 December 1871. Mr **Crowden** appeared before the Board and explained his treatment of the case of Mary **Roberts**. Unanimously resolved that in the opinion of this Board the explanation of D$^r$ Crowden is completely satisfactory. [Page 60]

27 December 1871. The Master reported he had taken £17-0-6 from John **Hudson** a pauper inmate. [Page 60]

27 December 1871. William **Fulcher** applied to the Guardians for the clothing of his daughter who had been maintained in the workhouse at the expense of the Union. Resolved that this man be allowed to have the clothes of his daughter Mary Ann without payment and that the master of the workhouse be requested to give them up accordingly. [Page 60]

8 January 1872. **Holland**. The Clerk reported that he attended the Magistrates Meeting and they had cancelled the Indentures of apprenticeship that the master was to return the sum of four pounds of the premium he had received but he was allowed to keep the clothes the Guardians to pay all expenses. The apprentice appeared before the Board and stated he now had no clothing except such as he had borrowed that he had no means of obtaining a supply. It was resolved that with the consent of the Local Government Board two pounds be allowed to Amos **Bennett** the discharged apprentice for clothing to wear the Magistrates having deprived him of it. [Page 63]

8 January 1872. Ordered that Frederick **Mallows** aged 24 years be summoned to show cause why he neglects to maintain his wife Emma Mallows and their two children who are now residing in the Workhouse and are chargeable to this Union and that R. O. **Marshall** procure the summons. [Page 65]

22 January 1872. **Bennett** Amos late apprentice to **Holland**. A letter dated 19$^{th}$ January 1872 numbered 2307A from the Local Government Board was read with reference to Amos Bennett being allowed £2 for clothing – the letter stated that before the Board could decide in the application of the Guardians, wish to be informed where the lad was, if he be in employment the Board presume that the earnings are sufficient to enable him to provide himself without assistance from the poor rate.

Resolved that the Local Government Board be informed that the lad is now with his uncle and is not at work but is wearing clothes belonging to his uncle and that he is unable to get work until clothes are provided and the uncle is not in a position to provide clothes and there has already been a delay of near three weeks. [Page 66]

22 January 1872. **Muckling** Frances. A letter from the Peterbro Union was read assenting to the relief of 6d extra per week to this pauper and requesting to be informed of the age and circumstances of the pauper and with whom she resides and whether any relative is able to contribute towards her support.

Resolved that the Guardians of the Peterborough Union be informed that she is 66 years of age nearly blind and resides by herself at Whaplode. That the sons are very poor sometimes having parish relief. [Page 67]

22 January 1872. The Guardians of the Spalding Union having written stating that Betsy **Childs** was now in their workhouse and is pregnant she is the daughter of John Childs of Gedney and has resided out of this Union from May last only. The Guardians also ask this Board to take her without orders of removal.

The case having been enquired into and the statement found correct Resolved that on Betsy Child being taken to the workhouse the master have instructions to admit her. [Page 67]

5 February 1872. Ordered that enquiries be made as to John **Childs** of Gedney coal dealer whether he is in a position to contribute towards the maintenance of his daughter. [Page 69]

5 February 1872. The Clerk reported the Local Government Board had consented to the payment of £2 for clothing for Amos **Bennett**, late apprentice to Mr **Holland**. [Page 69]

5 February 1872. **Crowson** [*blank*] having appeared before the Board and stated that under the advice of her uncle Henry **Lewis** a police constable at Whaplode Saint Andrew and by him brought into the Holbeach Union for the purpose of being confined Crowson having no means her uncle came with her and paid her railway fare she also stated she had no relative or friend in the Holbeach Union.

It is ordered that steps be taken for her removal to Holt the parish to which she belongs and that Henry Lewes be proceeded against for the illegal removal.

(The Collector of the Guardians after the Board had broken up and before a fair copy of these minutes were entered inquired of the pauper the particulars of the settlement and her for what purpose it was, she stated she would sooner leave the workhouse than be taken to Holt. She thereupon gave the master notice and forthwith quitted the house). [Page 71]

5 February 1872. Peterborough Union. Reported that Ann **French** with 3 children the relief is discontinued. Ann French being pregnant is unable to be removed the Guardians have ordered her to be removed to this workhouse and that the children are going to reside with the grandfather who is able to maintain them. [Page 71]

5 February 1872. John **Chamberlain** appeared before the Board and signed the Indenture of apprenticeship in the presence of the Guardians. [Page 73]

19 February 1872. **French** Ann. A letter dated the 10th instant from the Peterborough Board was read requesting that this pauper might be sent to their workhouse when in a fit state to be removed. Ordered that the matter be attended to. [Page 74]

19 February 1872. **Stevens** William Orders of removal from the Strand Union were read stating the above pauper had become chargeable. Ordered that he be received when brought to this Union. [Page 74]

19 February 1872. **Mackharness** Whaplode applies for his daughters clothing she is in the County Asylum he pays 2/6 weekly towards her maintenance – granted. [Page 74]

19 February 1872. Mr **Woods** proposed that inasmuch as Charlotte **Doncaster** late of Fleet Fen having died leaving a will by which she disposed of property of £10 to each daughter and the residue to her sons that a copy of the will be obtained with a view of reimbursing the Guardians one years relief.

Seconded by Mr **Corby** and unanimously carried. [Page 74]

19 February 1872. Ordered that enquiry be made as to the property of the late Mrs **Brown** who resided at Sutton Saint Edmunds, it being reported to this Board that the same is worth £12.12.0 per annum. There is a mortgage of £100 on this property should the statement be correct that steps be taken for the recovery of the relief advanced. [Page 74]

19 February 1872. That Thomas **Hales** and Sarah **Chamberlain** had signed John Chamberlains Indentures of apprenticeship. [Page 75]

4 March 1872. The Clerk reported that Emma **Smith** aged 42 years had been sent from the parish of Gedney to the County Asylum. [Page 79]

4 March 1872. **Lake**. Ordered that if Lake who has broke is settlement by residing in Moulton, applied for relief that he be removed to his place of settlement. [Page 80]

18 March 1872. The Relieving Officer reported he had obtained a warrant for the apprehension of [*blank*] **Dack** who had deserted his wife and two children. Approved. [Page 83]

15 April 1872. **Dack** W. Resolved that a further sum of three pounds do be paid the police towards their expenses in this matter. [Page 89]

15 April 1872. **Lawson** – the case of Sarah Lawson having been brought under the notice of the Board and it appearing that Mr **Crowden** by his medical report had visited only once during the past fortnight viz on the 5th instant and given medicine on the 6th instant and the case being a serious nature the Guardians are desirous that Mr Crowden should render some explanation his attention having been called to the case on the first instant. [Page 90]

15 April 1872. Resolved that William **Chartes** be sent to London for the purpose of Messrs **Ferguson** supplying him with a proper truss for his rupture. [Page 90]

15 April 1872. Resolved that Rosanna **Gardner** have proper instruments for straightening her legs. [Page 90]

15 April 1872. Apprentice. – Mr **Wright** of Sutton Saint Edmunds applies to have Benjamin **Johnson** as an apprentice to learn the trade of a shoemaker.
Resolved that D$^r$ **Harper** examine the boy as to his fitness to learn the trade and if found fit the application be granted. [Page 90]

15 April 1872. The wife of John **Richards** Miller and Baker at Whaplode Drove applied to the Board for advice as to his daughter aged 26 years M$^{rs}$ Richards stating she was of unsound mind. M$^r$ Richards is part owner of a Steam Mill. [Page 90]

29 April 1872. Mr Vincent **Eastgate** applied to the Guardians for the purpose of having his contract as to Harriett **Green** rescinded the Aunt of the Child having obtained a better situation for her – granted. [Page 95]

13 May 1872. **Lawson** Sarah. A letter from Mr **Crowden** was read with reference to this case.
Also a letter from M$^r$ **Faulkner** charging Mr Crowden with neglecting the case of Sarah Lawson.
Resolved that each party have a copy of each others letters and that Mr Crowden be requested to attend at the next meeting of the Guardians and that M$^r$ Faulkner be requested to attend to substantiate his charges. [Page 97]

13 May 1872. **Culy** Benjamin wife and two children. The Guardians of the Ashby de la Zouch Union having written stating this party belongs to Whaplode and that Culy was permanently disabled, and is receiving 4/- and 12lb bread weekly and asking this Board to confirm the relief in order to save expenses of removal orders.
Order that the Clerk write and inquire how long Culy has resided in that Union also the ages of the children. [Page 97]

13 May 1872. Ordered that Susan **Wignal** have a cast of her foot taken in London. [Page 97]

27 May 1872. **Richards** a lunatic. Ordered that Mr. Richards be requested to attend the next meeting of the Guardians with reference to his daughters maintenance in the asylum. [Page 100]

27 May 1872. Benjamin **Johnson** 14 years having been on trial at Mr. Henry **Wright**s of Sutton St. Edmunds for a period of six weeks and the master and Johnson both appearing before the Board stated they were satisfied with each other It was resolved to bind Johnson to Mr. Wright for a period of 5 years to learn the art of a shoemaker also to pay a premium of £12. [Page 100]

27 May 1872. Frances **Skinn**. That the Clerk issue a Summons against William Stainton Skinn of Fleet for neglecting to maintain his Grandchildren returnable at the next meeting at Long Sutton. [Page 100]

10 June 1872. **Johnson** Benjamin aged 14 years belonging to Long Sutton. Mr. **Blower** one of the Trustees of Allens Charity stated that the charity could not obtain a sufficient number of Boys to apprentice and that the trustees were willing to apprentice Johnson.
Ordered that Mr. **Wright** the master be informed thereof also that the premium allowed by the Charity is £25. [Bound *written in margin*] [Page 102]

10 June 1872. Mr. John **Richards** of Whaplode Drove appeared before the Board with reference to the maintenance of his daughter. He stated as follows – that he could not afford to pay more than 5/- weekly towards the maintenance of his daughter. He had ¾ of land, a steam mill running one pair french and one pair of Grey Stones a House and bakehouse all his own property subject to mortgage of <u>about</u> £14 per annum [*in the margin in pencil* he would not say the exact amount] the engine is a ten horse power. The Mill runs one day per week at grist work and charges 8$^d$ per bushel baker 9 sacks per week. Some of the Guardians were of opinion that Mr. Richards is in a position to maintain his daughter in the county asylum.
Mr. **Boor** proposed that the amount remain at 5/- weekly towards the maintenance of his daughter.
Seconded by the Rev$^d$ J. L. **Bennett**.
It being put to the vote there appeared for the proposition 5 against it 9.
The proposition being lost It was resolved that Mr. Richards pay the full amount and he being present was informed thereof. [Page 102]

10 June 1872. A letter from the Local Government Board was read (N$^o$ 28746A dated 27$^{th}$ May 1872) also a copy of a letter from Thomas **Ward** of Tydd Saint Mary requesting to be furnished with the observations of the Guardians on Ward's communication which stated the Guardians had taken off his allowance of three shillings weekly that he was living with his daughter who had to maintain her two children and herself.

Resolved that the Local Government Board be informed that the reason the relief was discontinued is the immoral character of the daughter with whom he lives and the filthy condition of the house. [Page 104]

10 June 1872. Mary **Clarke** and children being now in the Union Workhouse and deserted It is ordered that a warrant be obtained for the husbands apprehension. [Page 106]

24 June 1872. **Betts** Ann. It being reported to this Board that Ann Betts (who had deserted her children and who are now chargeable to this Union) is residing at Norwich or Newton near to Norwich. It is ordered that a warrant be obtained for her apprehension and the usual reward of one guinea be given for her apprehension. [Page 108]

24 June 1872. James **Lake** aged 76 Settlement Gedney. Resolved that this man be allowed to reside at Moulton Chapel with his son Thomas Lake and that 3/- weekly be paid him through the Spalding Union. [Page 109]

24 June 1872. Resolved that Francis **Hyde** the son of Ann Hyde residing at Long Sutton be allowed 30/- and for clothing and his railway fare to Mansfield in consequence of Allens charity allowing him £25 to apprentice him to a carpenter and that the Local Government Board be requested to sanction this payment. [Page 109]

8 July 1872. **Hydes** Francis. A letter dated 29th June 1872 from the Local Government Board was read enquiring whether Francis Hyde was in the workhouse and whether his mother was receiving relief.
Ordered that the Clerk report that neither Francis Hyde or his mother are in receipt of relief. [Page 111]

8 July 1872. Ordered that a Warrant be obtained by R. O. **Marshall** for the apprehension of [*blank*] **Sharpe** for deserting her children and the usual reward offered – that the Seal of the Board be affixed to Marshalls authority. [Page 111]

8 July 1872. Medical Officer **Harper** recommended that Hannah **Sweeney** aged 21 years and suffering from Rheumatism be sent to Buxton Baths.
The Chairman stated that Doctor Harper had recommended him to take Lemon Juice when he suffered from a similar complaint and from which Lemon juice he had received great benefit.
Ordered that the Clerk write to Doctor Harper suggesting a trial of lemon juice for the above pauper. [Page 112]

8 July 1872. **Winkley** John aged 75 residence Holbeach applied to the Board to be relieved at Peakhill in the Spalding Union. He was going to reside with his son in law Isaac **Wilson**.
Ordered that the clerk write to the Guardians of the Spalding Union asking them to relieve Winkley with 3/- weekly and charge the same to this Union. [Page 112]

22 July 1872. **Hyde** Francis (pa 111). A letter from the Local Government Board dated 18th July 1872 was read stating the Guardians cannot apply the poor rates in the manner proposed in relieving the above pauper. [Page 115]

22 July 1872. **King** Rebecca Settlement Holbeach – aged 56 years. This pauper being about to reside at Clapham Common it is resolved that she be allowed 3/6 weekly provided the Guardians of the Union in which that parish is situate will administer the relief. [Page 116]

2 September 1872. A letter from the Local Government Board dated 23rd August 1872 stating that the last return form A contained the statement that "there are four children in the workhouse unvaccinated one of whom has been in the house four years" and they had also heard from Doctor **Beard** (one of the Inspectors of Vaccination) that when he visited the workhouse on the 28th May last a boy named James **Jackson** aged eight years had not been vaccinated. The Local Government Board enquired whether the case referred to in form A be that of James Jackson also the age of each of the other children referred to.
Ordered that the Clerk inform the Local Government Board that the above named James Jackson is the Boy referred to in Doctor Beards Report and that Mr. **Goddard** reported on the 30 May 1870 as under
"The children appear clean and generally healthy. I have examined the arms of all and found that Vaccination has been performed in every case". The boy was in the workhouse at that date the age of the other children are 9 weeks 5 weeks and two weeks respectively & the boy has since been vaccinated. [Page 125]

16 September 1872. Resolved that the Clerk take out a Summons against William **Goodwin** of Long Sutton Ratcatcher for the payment of 1/6 weekly towards the maintenance of the child of Sarah **Bennett** of which child he was adjudged to be the father on the second April 1869. [Page 132]

16 September 1872. Resolved that the Clerk take out a Summons against John **Richards** of Whaplode Drove Miller and Baker for the amount of maintenance of his daughter in the county Asylum at Bracebridge. [Page 132]

16 September 1872. The Master reported that the child John **Walker** born in the workhouse and now aged [blank] had not been registered.
Resolved that the Clerk write to the Local Government Board enquiring whether the Registrar of Births and deaths are bound to attend at the Union see article N° 208 sub article 13. [Page 134]

30 September 1872. **Richards** John. The Clerk reported he had appeared before the Justices in this case for the payment of the costs of Mr Richards daughter in the Lincoln County Asylum and from the statements there made he withdrew the summons.
Ordered that the Collector take out a Summons against John Richards to recover the 5/- per week agreed to be paid by him provided he does not at once pay that sum and that the seal of the Board be affixed to the Authority (to the Collector) and signed by the Chairman. [Page 136]

30 September 1872. Aston Union. A letter from this union dated the 27th September 1872 was read asking this Board to take Sarah **Woods** and her child without orders of removal. Sarah Woods from the statement sent is 39 years of age and was married to Robt Woods at Childerwal – Lancaster on 5th April 1852 she and her child was deserted at Mount Street Nechells Aston (the child is 9 years of age and is a cripple) in June 1871 and became chargeable on the 28 Sept 1871 and are now chargeable – the husband is the illegitimate child of Rebecca Woods and was born in the workhouse of Sutton St Eds his grandfather James Woods resided in Guanock Gate in their own freehold.
Resolved that the Guardians do not feel themselves justified in receiving this pauper and that the Guardians of the Aston Union be informed thereof accordingly. [Page 137]

14 October 1872. Mr **Haines** reported as to Wm **Hicks** that he intended to take off the porter and watch the effect and if he gets worse to put it on again.
**Harvey.** Mr Haines reported that this man had been removed to the workhouse. [Page 144]

28 October 1872. A letter from Dr **Crowden** was read applying to be allowed £1.1.0 in the case of [blank] **Andrews** for cutting out a tumour by which he was enabled to continue at work and his health improved. The pain of the tumour was so great as to affect his health and prevent his sleeping and had it not been cut off he would have been entirely dependent on relief.
Resolved that Mr. Crowden be allowed £1.1.0 in this case and that the same be reported to the Local Government Board for their approval. [Page 145]

11 November 1872. The following letters from the Local Government Board were read:
59008 dated 4th November 1872 sanctioning the payment of the sum of £1.1.0 to Mr. James Trigue **Crowden** for **Andrews** surgical operation.
58995 dated 5th November 1872 sanctioning the payment of the sum of £2.2.0 to Mr. A. B. **Vise** for a surgical operation performed upon William **Garner.** [Page 148]

11 November 1872. Ordered that the Clerk apply to Mr. William **Naylor** of Whaplode enquiring the position of Mrs Elizth **Sharpe** an inmate to maintain her children out of her late husbands property (George Sharpe died 14 Sept. 1871). [Page 148]

25 November 1872. **Smith** John. A letter from the Revd James **Jerram** of Fleet requesting the Guardians to again investigate the matter as to **Fulford** being in the family way by John Smith.
The Guardians investigated the matter and are perfectly satisfied with their former decision. [Page 151]

25 November 1872. **Aucock** William Settlement Gedney. This pauper having gone to reside at Wisbech and having informed this Board that the Guardians of the Wisbech Union were willing to pay 3/- weekly on behalf of this Union.
Ordered that the Clerk write to the Wisbech Union that if such is the fact that the relief be paid. [Page 151]

25 November 1872. **Rickett** Sarah. Ordered that Medical Officer **Vise** to report as to her permanent disability and should she be permanently disabled that the clerk ask the Spalding Union to take her without orders of removal. [Page 152]

9 December 1872. In the indoor Medical report book there is the following report:
"I find that the Boys **Clarke, Wignall, Jackson, Brace, Sharpe** and **Bills** have for ten nights been applying a flannel dipped in <u>urine</u> to their heads and covering the same with a handkerchief or cloth to prevent evaporation and that they have done the same at the recommendation of the Barber, a more <u>filthy</u> or <u>pernicious</u> system could not be adopted and I trust measures will be taken to prevent this person or any other or any other from interfering with any patient for the future. It was this that accounted for the urinous smell when the Inspector of Schools went round the wards at his recent visit."

The Schoolmaster under whose care these children were explained that he was not aware of the above proceedings and the man Sharpe who superintended the children said it was done at the suggestion of Mr **Bell** the Barber.

Resolved that Mr Bell be requested to confine himself to the duties of his contract and not interfere with the management of the paupers. [Page 154]

23 December 1872. Mr. **Hales** of Crowland sent his apprentice John **Chamberlain** to appear before the Board pursuant to the Covenant in the Indenture. Chamberlain expressed himself well satisfied with his place. [Page 157]

6 January 1873. **Bennett**s bastard children. Unanimously Resolved that the question why the order obtained (on the thirty first October) upon **Goodwin** had not been properly issued by the Clerk of the Justices. [Page 161]

6 January 1873. **Wilkinson**. A letter from the Hornsey District with reference to Mr **Watts** position to maintain the Boy the officers stated the man was out of work and in his opinion the lad was better where he is.
Ordered that Watts be written to asking him what his position is and as to the boys education. [Page 161]

6 January 1873. Resolved that M$^r$ Robert **Leaver** the secretary of the Long Sutton Benefit Society be applied to for the maintenance of the late John **Burton** who was an inmate of this workhouse. [Page 162]

6 January 1873. Ordered that the Clerk enquire into the settlement of Emma **Rippin** aged 20 years now an inmate of this workhouse. [Page 162]

6 January 1873. Mr Matthew **Gott** applied to have a relative viz Susannah **Dolson** for a weeks visit – Granted. [Page 162]

6 January 1873. **Amory** Fanny aged 35 years residing at Gedney Hill. Ordered that the Clerk write to the Local Government Board and ask if the Guardians can relieve her she being partially paralized – a single woman she having had three bastard children one of which is more dependent. [Page 162]

20 January 1873. **Wilkinson** – Mr **Walls** having written stating he was a Smith and Farrier by trade but did not state whether he was in work. Resolved that if on further enquiry it is found that Watts is in a position to maintain his nephew that the boy Wilkinson be taken to Hornsey to his uncle. [Page 165]

3 February 1873. Resolved that inasmuch as William **Goodwin** has not paid the sum ordered to be paid by the Justices in Sarah **Bennett**s case that the Collector proceed against him for the recovery thereof and that the usual authority be signed and the Seal of the Board affixed thereto. [Page 167]

3 February 1873. Ordered that the Clerk write to Zephaniah **Bradley** of Bourn tailer and John Bradley of Louth Watch Maker and ask them what sum they are willing to contribute towards the maintenance of their mother. [Page 167]

3 February 1873. **Ewen** William to be removed to write as above first Setchford. [Page 167]

3 February 1873. Ordered that the Guardians of the Whittlesey Union be written to asking them to take Samuel **Christopher** without orders of removal under the following circumstances for he was born in the parish of Coates about 61 years ago and when he attained the age of 17 years he let himself to John **Boyce** of Whittlesey as an hired servant for a period of a whole year and served the whole of that time, that he also continued in the same service. [Page 168]

3 February 1873. Resolved that the Collector take **Wilkinson** and [blank] to their respective places of service. [Page 168]

17 February 1873. **King** Rebecca. A letter from M$^{rs}$ **Mellor** of Clapham Common stating that Rebecca King had fallen down and broken her wrist and was unable to do anything for herself.

Resolved that a Nurse be allowed and M^rs Mellor advanced money to pay for the same. [Page 169]

17 February 1873. **Allwood** George. Medical Officer **Harper** reported that George Allwood would be much benefitted by a residence at Margate Infirmary in the summer.

Resolved that Dr Harper be requested to give his reasons for wishing the above also the method of obtaining admission into the infirmary and the cost of maintenance. [Page 170]

17 February 1873. **Sweeney** Hannah. D^r Harper suggested that Hannah Sweeney should be sent to the Buxton Hospital

Resolved that an order be obtained when the weather admits of her being sent to the hospital. [Page 170]

3 March 1873. Resolved that orders of removal be taken out for the removal of William **Ewen** and Samuel **Christopher** and that the usual authority for the Clerk to proceed therein be signed by the Chairman and the Seal of the Board affixed thereto. [*In the margin* One sent away order received for the other] [Page 172]

3 March 1873. **Cardell** W^m A Lunatic. A letter from the Grantham Union dated 15 Feby 1873 was read stating that William Cardell a Lunatic and belongs to Whaplode and asking whether this Board would acknowledge and pay the expenses of his removal to Bracebridge. [Page 173]

3 March 1873. **Stokes** Ann widow. A letter dated 27 February 1873 from the Lincoln Union was read stating that Ann Stokes and her two children had gone to reside in the parish of Barlings in the Lincoln Union that her husband died the 7 June 1872 at Doncaster and whose mother had been removed to Whaplode in this Union. Also asking this Board to relieve with 3/- weekly.

No order made in either of the above cases. [Page 173]

17 March 1873. Ordered that the Clerk write to the Spalding Union requesting them to sanction 6^d additional relief to John **Pidd** a pauper chargeable to that Union. [Page 179]

17 March 1873. Resolved that the mother of Edward **Bett** who died in the workhouse be allowed to take her sons clothes. [Page 179]

17 March 1873. Resolved that John **Wilson** be apprenticed to Jabez **Adams** of Holbeach Baker to go on trial for one month. [Page 180]

17 March 1873. Ordered that William Payling **Hotchen** of Fleet Fen Farmer be called upon to pay for the maintenance of his son William Hotchen. [Page 180]

17 March 1873. That William **Ewen** had been removed to Docking Union pursuant to the order of the last Meeting of the Guardians. [Page 180]

31 March 1873. John **Walker** of Whaplode applied to have William **Wignal** of Holbeach as an apprentice as a brick layer – ordered that Wignal go on one months trial. [Page 183]

31 March 1873. Ordered that Medical Officer **Ewen** be requested to report on the case of John **Butcher** of Gedney Dike. [Page 183]

31 March 1873. **Hardy** Harriet – Back Lane Long Sutton – Ordered that this pauper be removed to her settlement. [Page 183]

31 March 1873. **Triffett** Jeremiah, Holbeach, Saddler – Resolved that M^r Triffitt be requested to attend the next meeting of the Guardians to show cause why he does not contribute towards the maintenance of his father and mother (John and Ann **Trifitt**). [Page 183]

31 March 1873. **Rickett**. Ordered that the Clark report to the Spalding Union that this pauper has gone to reside in the Horncastle Union. [Page 183]

14 April 1873. Peterborough Union – **French** Ann – The Guardians of the Peterboro Union having requested this Board to pay this pauper 4/6 per week for nine weeks. [Page 188]

14 April 1873. **Triffett** Jeremiah appeared before the Board and stated he was not in a position to contribute towards the maintenance of his father and mother that his income was only £107 per annum and that he paid £16 rent kept one apprentice. [*In margin* Wifes earning £55 himself & apprentice as a saddler 52 = £107]

Resolved that Triffitt be summoned before the Justices to show cause why he does not contribute towards the support of his parents. [Page 188]

14 April 1873. Resolved W^m **Hodgkinson** be summoned to show cause why he refuses to contribute towards the maintenance of his father. [Page 188]

14 April 1873. **Whiley** John aged 80 settlement Whaplode – Ordered that the Guardians of the Lynn Union be asked to pay to this pauper 3/- weekly and charge the same to this Union. [Page 189]

## EXTRACTS FROM THE HOLBEACH UNION WORKHOUSE MINUTES
### PL8/102/19 1871 - 1873

14 April 1873. M$^r$ **Adams** appeared before the Board and asked the Guardians to have John **Wilson** aged 12 years bound to him as an apprentice until he attains the age of 18 years.

Resolved that M$^r$ Adams apply again next Board day and in the mean time he is to attend at the Clerks office and read the usual form of Indenture. [Page 189]

28 April 1873. **Stokes** Ann and two children aged respectively 2 years and 7 mo – Settlement Whaplode – A letter from the Lincoln Union was read asking this Board to relieve with 3/- weekly. Resolved that the Lincoln Board be requested to relieve and charge the same in the usual way. [Page 194]

28 April 1873. **Guymer** Ann. Resolved that the husband of this pauper be apprehended for deserting her and her two children and that one pound reward be given. [Page 195]

28 April 1873. Mr **Adams** appeared before the Board and agreed to take John **Wilson** as an apprentice until he attains the age of 18 years. [Page 196]

12 May 1873. **Hotchinson.** The Clerk reported that this case had been adjourned until the 20 instant and Mr **Winfrey** suggested the following witnesses [Page 197]

> The father of the deft [*defendant*]
>
> Mr **Franks**
>
> Mr Winfrey

12 May 1873. Ordered that the Clerk write to the Spalding Union asking them to put on 6$^d$ additional to John **Pidd** a pauper chargeable to that Union

Also 6$^d$ per week additional to Mary **Woodward**. [Page 198]

26 May 1873. The Clerk reported that the Guardians of the Spalding Union had confirmed the payment of 6d per week additional to **Pidd** and **Woodward** two paupers relieved by this Union on behalf of the Spalding Union. [Page 199]

26 May 1873. M$^r$ **Harper** being present suggested that Jeremiah **Triffitt** should be furnished with a Patten shoe.

Resolved that a shoe be purchased for Triffitt. [Page 199]

26 May 1873. Mr **Harper** (Workhouse Medical Officer) suggested that George **Atwood** now in the infirmary suffering from Abscess would be benefitted by going to the Sea Bathing Infirmary.

Ordered that the Clerk write to the Secretary of the Sea Bathing Infirmary Margate asking for Attwoods admission into that establishment. [Page 200]

26 May 1873. Ordered that the Clerk write to the Luton Union informing them that Catharine **Holland** is no longer receiving relief she having gone into service. [Page 200]

26 May 1873. John **Wilson** born 14$^{th}$ April 1860 was bound apprentice to M$^r$ Jabez **Adams** baker of Holbeach for a term of five years the Indentures were signed by Mr Adams and J. Wilson in the presence of the Guardians and the Seal of the Board affixed by Mr. **Crawley.** [Page 201]

9 June 1873. **Atwood** George – Application having been made to the Margate Infirmary for the admission of this pauper into that establishment – the secretary reported that on the male side there would be no vacancies for a considerable time – the subscription would be £5 for a bed and 6/- per week maintenance exclusive of washing – no order made. [Page 201]

9 June 1873. **Eagle** Emma – Mr Thomas **Bell** butcher of Whaplode applied to have Emma Eagle aged 13 years & from the parish of Gedney as a domestic servant. Resolved that an outfit to the amount of £1 15 0 be allowed and that £1.15.0 be the wages for one year. Ordered that R. O. **Marshall** be requested to visit Emma Eagle pursuant to Sec 4 14 &15 Vic cap 11. [Page 210]

9 June 1873. Peterborough Union – Ordered that the Clerk write to the Peterboro Union informing them that Ann **French** W$^o$ (and whose relief they repay) is now pregnant. [Page 202]

9 June 1873. M$^{rs}$ **Lake** applied for her brother-in-laws clothing he having died in the workhouse and the friends having buried him at their own cost – Granted. [Page 202]

9 June 1873. Mr **Temple** of Gedney shopkeeper by his wife applied to have Richard **Bridgeman** of Gedney aged 86 years admitted into the workhouse he not having the means to maintain himself and being a relative of Mr Temple but not bound by law to maintain him. Mrs Temple stated her husband was willing to pay 3/6 per week. Resolved that Bridgeman be admitted – that Mr Temple be requested to sign the usual agreement. [Page 202]

23 June 1873. The Master reported that Mess$^s$ **Bush** of Long Sutton had applied to have Louisa **Betts** as a Domestic Servant. Resolved that inasmuch as Louisa Betts has attained the age of 14 years and being deserted by her mother that she be allowed to go to Mess$^s$ Bush on trial for a period of one month. [Page 205]

23 June 1873. **Winkley** a pauper in the Spalding Union the Guardians of that Union reported by letter dated the 20 June that they had given 6$^d$ per week additional to Winkley approved. [Page 208]

7 July 1873. **Hart** Joseph. Ordered that a warrant be obtained by the master for the apprehension of Joseph **Sharpe** [sic] for deserting his three children viz William aged 7 years or thereabouts Elizabeth aged 5 years or thereabouts and John aged 3 or thereabouts. [Page 210]

7 July 1873. Ordered that the Clerk write to the Guardians of the Grantham Union enquiring whether Mr [blank] **Chambers** is a proper place to send Mary Ann **Hicks** aged 15 years as a domestic servant and should the reply be satisfactory R. O. **Marshall** is to provide clothing to the amount of 30/-. [Page 211]

7 July 1873. Mary **Haylock** aged 66 widow of John Haylock lighterman had relief about two years from Ely Union is now living with her son in law = ask the Ely Union to allow 2/9 per week. [Page 211]

21 July 1873. Resolved that Thomas **Harrison** be summoned for neglecting to maintain his wife and child (he having given only 11/6 on the 12$^{th}$ instant and refusing to give her any further sum and the woman at the recommendation of the Rev$^d$ E. L. **Bennett** having come into the workhouse) and that the summons be returnable at the next meeting of the Magistrates at Long Sutton. [Page 213]

4 August 1873. The quarterly return of Lunatics was read – and on such return appeared the name of Ellen **Hipkin** and one of the Guardians remarking Hipkin was at Long Sutton. It is ordered that the Clerk enquire whether she has been discharged from the Asylum or escaped therefrom no notice being sent to the officers of this Union. [Page 215]

4 August 1873. Lunacy. – **Arnsby** Elizabeth the Guardians of the Saint Ives Union having written that this pauper was paralysed and prostrate It is Resolved that the matter be left entirely in the hands of the Guardians of the Saint Ives Union to deal with the matter as they may think proper. [Page 215]

18 August 1873. It was reported to the Board that James **Rump** aged 46 years from the parish of Lutton had been sent to the County Asylum. [Page 217]

18 August 1873. Wisbech Union **Harber** Thomas aged 73 years chargeable to the Wisbech Union. The Guardians of that Union asks this Board by letter to take the pauper without orders of the removal under the following circumstances viz that he became chargeable to that Union in July last – he hired the White Lyon at Tydd Saint Mary for £20 per annum and remained tenant from March 1871 to Lady day 1873 – he paid one years rent and all rates and taxes. Ordered that enquiries be made into the matter and report thereon next Board day. [Page 217]

18 August 1873. Mr **Vise** having given cod liver oil to Charles **Fletcher** of Whaplode and had omitted to enter same on his report. Ordered that Mr Vise be written to requesting him to enter extras ordered by him, on his report. [218]

18 August 1873. Mr **Harper** having omitted to enter the name of James **Cunnington** on his report and the case appearing of a serious nature. Order that Mr Harper be requested to enter the paupers name in his reports. [Page 218]

1 September 1873. **Nidd** and family Braintree Union. Resolved that enquiries be made into this case so that the relief may be revised. [Page 220]

1 September 1873. **Sweeney** Hannah aged 22 years suffering from rheumatic gout is desirous of being sent to Buxton. Resolved that she be sent should Mr **Harper** think it a proper case and if so that he furnish this Board with the necessary information to send her there. [Page 220]

1 September 1873. The wife of John **Scott** formerly of Sutton Saint Edmunds applied to this Board for relief – refused – And the Clerk write John Scott that if his wife becomes chargeable to this Union through his neglect to maintain her the Guardians will at once procure a warrant for his apprehension. [Page 220]

1 September 1873. A letter from Ashby de la Zouch Union was read asking this board to relieve Sarah **Culy** and her two children the Guardians not being satisfied with the particulars stated as to Settlement decline to accede to the request. [Page 223]

1 September 1873. Wisbech Union **Harber** Thomas enquiries having been made as to the Settlement – and finding the statement correct – the Clerk is ordered to inform the Wisbech Board that on Harber being sent to this Union Workhouse the Master has instructions to admit him. [Page 223]

15 September 1873. **Nidd** and family no report having been received from the Braintree Union as to the family of this pauper and the Guardians of this Union being of opinion that the family must by this time be able to earn something towards a livelihood It is resolved that this relief be reduced 2/- weekly. [Page 224]

15 September 1873. **Filer** widow – A letter N° 56612A – dated 4th Sept 1873 from Local Government Board – accompanied with a letter purporting to be from Mr Joseph **Woodward** of Holbeach with reference to the relief being taken off Widow Filer.

Resolved that the Local Government Board be – in reply to their letter – informed that the Guardians having several times had the matter before them are fully satisfied with their decision. The widow Filer has applied to the Local Board of Health at Holbeach to have the house in which she resides registered as a common Lodging house but they do not feel justified in registering it. There are only two bed rooms & one of them very small. The house has no separate privy accommodation it is assessed to the poor rate at £2-15-0 only. The Inspector of Police having reason to think that a person was in the house whom he wanted caused the house to be searched he found two women sleeping with one man and owing to the great age viz 75 years of widow Filer she is not a proper person to keep a lodging house & they do not feel justified under the circumstances of granting relief. [Page 224]

29 September 1873. **Westmoreland** George. Ordered that he be requested to attend the next meeting of the Board to show cause why he does not maintain his father. [Page 229]

29 September 1873. **Nidd** and family. The Clerk of the Braintree Union having written stating there was now only four children viz John aged 14 years earning 1/- per week and 6 days food Robert aged 11 years earning 2/- weekly – Mary 9 years & Edward 7 years both at school – Richard aged 19 had been left 2 years and Russell aged 16 had left her 2 years. Ordered that the Clerk inform Mr **Cunnington** that this Board must discontinue relief. [Page 229]

29 September 1873. Mr **Arnold** of Fleet having applied to have Edward **Wilkinson** an orphan aged 14 years as an apprentice to the trade of a shoemaker. Resolved that Edward Wilkinson be allowed to go a month on trial. [Page 229]

13 October 1873. **Westmoreland** George appeared before the Board and stated he was unable to maintain his father – he occupied 10 acres of land for £50 – but upon enquiry it appeared he had of

| | | | | | |
|---|---|---|---|---|---|
| Mrs **Horry** | 3a | 2a | 5 | for | 18.0.0 |
| Mr **Tinsley** | 7 | 2 | 13 | for | 28.0 0 |
| | 11 | 0 | 18 | | 46.0.0 |

That he also kept a beerhouse and lodging house and had no family to maintain. Resolved that Westmoreland pay 2/6 per week towards the maintenance of his parents and should he be in arrears for more than two weeks that he be summoned. [Page 1]

13 October 1873. Luton Union **Holland** Catharine relief paid by the Guardians of the said Union – Ordered that the Clerk write and ask that Board to allow 15/- Clothing that pauper having gone out to service. [Page 1]

13 October 1873. **Nidd** Emma – Braintree applied by letter to be relieved where she is now residing. Ordered that if Braintree Union will relieve this Board will repay them but the Guardians cannot consistently relieve through private individuals and that M$^{rs}$ Nidd be requested to apply to the Guardians of the Braintree Union. [Page 1]

13 October 1873. **Eagle** Emma aged 13 years residing with Mr **Bell** asks permission to take Eagle to Sheffield. Granted. [Page 1]

27 October 1873. Mr **Arnold** shoemaker Fleet applied to have Edward **Wilkinson** an orphan bound apprentice to him. The Guardians offered £12 premium, Mr Arnold wanted the Guardians to clothe the boy in addition this not being in accordance with the regulations he declined to take him. [Page 3]

27 October 1873. Mr David **Smith** baker applied to have the above named Edward **Wilkinson** a month on trial. It was resolved the application be granted. [Page 3]

27 October 1873. The usual Authority was signed authorizing the Clerk to summon **Westmoreland** for not maintaining his father. [Page 3]

27 October 1873. **Harper** Rob$^t$. Medical Report – It appeared that in **Smalley** family he had omitted to enter 3lbs mutton 1 bottle wine 7 pints Porter and in the following week 3lbs mutton 7 pints Ale. And in the case of Matthew **Towns** 1 bottle wine and the dates omitted. Ordered that the clerk write M$^r$ Harper thereon. [Page 3]

10 November 1873. **Nidd** and family. The Clerk of the Braintree Union reported they had requested their relieving officer to enquire into the case. [Page 5]

10 November 1873. Lunacy. The Clerk reported that Ann **Butcher** had been discharged from the asylum on the 4$^{th}$ instant. [Page 5]

10 November 1873. Mary Ann **Eagle** having deserted her illegitimate child Joseph Eagle aged 3 years by leaving him with Thomas **Brightman** of Fleet Fen and which said child is now in the workhouse. Ordered Ann Eagle be apprehended and an authority signed by the Chairman be given to the Clerk to take proceedings. [Page 5]

10 November 1873. **Hunt** John 8 Wentworth Road East Greenwich having with his wife neglected to maintain Mary Ann **Collins** the illegitimate child of the wife of the said John Hunt and the Guardians having allowed 1/6 per week towards the maintenance of the child It is ordered that Hunt be summoned to show cause why he omits to maintain the child – and an Authority to the Clark be signed to take the necessary proceedings. [Page 5]

24 November 1873. **Rogers**. Resolved that an authority be given under the Seal of the Board for the master John W. **Hart** to prosecute Susanna Rogers for neglecting to maintain her bastard child. [Page 7]

24 November 1873. **Walpole** R$^t$. Resolved that should the Master ascertain where Robert Walpole can be found that he prosecute the said Robert Walpole for neglecting to maintain his mother Sarah Walpole now an inmate of the Union Workhouse and the Seal of the Board be affixed to the authority. [Page 7]

24 November 1873. **Hunt** John. Ordered that enquiries be made as to whether John Hunt is now residing at No 8 Wentworth road East Greenwich and that the usual reward be given for his apprehension. [Page 7]

24 November 1873. Boston Union. Ordered that the Guardians of the Boston Union be informed that Mary Stanley **Rogers** will be admitted into this workhouse on a certificate being produced that she is not suffering from temporary disability. [Page 7]

8 December 1873. Lynn Union. The Guardians of the Lynn Union having written asking this Board to accept John **Whiley** without orders of removal (that Union having relieved him on behalf of this Union) stating the pauper was now in their workhouse. Resolved that an order for his admission be sent. [Page 9]

8 December 1873. **Skinn** W. S. not having paid anything towards the maintenance of his Grand children Resolved that an execution be applied for against his goods for the amount due. [Page 9]

8 December 1873. **Rudkin** Sarah – The master reported that M$^{rs}$ **Ayliff** had applied for this Girl as a housemaid. Unanimously Resolved that the application be granted. [Page 9]

8 December 1873. **Clay** William – This boy being brought to the Union Workhouse for the convenience of the Medical Officer attending a serious case it is Resolved that his father Clarke Clay pay 4/- per week towards his maintenance (Lundys farm?). [reduced to 3/- 22 Dec 1873 *in margin*] [Page 10]

8 December 1873. **Stewart** Henry now having two shilling weekly belongs to the Walsingham Union. Ordered that the Clerk write to that Union asking them to relieve here. [Page 10]

8 December 1873. **Hunt** John No 2 Whitworth Street East Greenwich. Ordered that the Clerk write him to fetch the child to his own home or maintain it elsewhere than at the cost of this Union. [Page 10]

8 December 1873. Ordered that the Clerk request Mr Anthony **Fysh** to appear before this Board for the purpose of making some arrangement for contributing towards the maintenance of his mother. [Page 11]

22 December 1873. W$^{m}$ Stainton **Skinn** applied to the Board to have the amount contributed by him reduced from 7/6 per week towards the maintenance of his Grandchildren he stated to the Guardians his position he having paid £5. Resolved that the payments be reduced to 3/- weekly from the 7$^{th}$ day of October 1872 but the order of Justices is not to be withdrawn. [Page 13]

22 December 1873. **Fysh** Anthony. Gedney – Mr Fysh appeared before the Board and signed an agreement to repay to this Board 2/- weekly towards the maintenance of his mother Ellen **Pollin** widow. [Page 13]

22 December 1873. **Panks** William Freebridge Union. The relief of this pauper being discontinued in consequence of his earning 5/- weekly and neglecting to attend school the uncle of the boy sent him to this Union. Resolved that the Guardians of the Freebridge Union be asked to admit William Panks into their Workhouse on his being sent there. [Page 13]

5 January 1874. **Fysh** Anthony writes to say he is unable to pay 2/- weekly M$^{r}$ Wm **Franks** and the Guardians for Gedney having explained Fysh's position M$^{r}$ Franks gave notice that he would move at the next meeting of the Board that the Contract entered into by Fysh be rescinded. Ordered that the Collector in the mean time do not enforce the payments under Fysh's contract. [Page 15]

5 January 1874. **Hunt - Collins** Rebecca of No 3 Orchard Road Plumstead Woolwich having written stating she was not married to Hunt and that she had another child and that she would provide for the child now chargeable and asking the Guardians to wait a short time to enable her to do so. Resolved that the matter stand over until the next meeting of the Guardians. [Page 15]

5 January 1874. Fakenham Union re **Stewart** Henry – A letter dated the 29 instant was received from the Fakenham Union stating it was against their rules to give relief to non resident poor also stating that on Stewart being taken to their workhouse he would be admitted. Resolved that Stewart be sent to that Union. [Page 15]

5 January 1874. **Hart** Joseph. Resolved that an Authority be given to the Master to take out a warrant for the apprehension of Joseph Hart labourer of Long Sutton for deserting his children. [Page 15]

5 January 1874. Lincoln Union – **Walton** James 26 years of age a Lunatic. A letter from the Lincoln [*Union*] was read stating that this pauper had been discharged from a London Hospital, that he had been removed to the County Asylum and he belonging to this Union they ask this Board to take him without orders of removal. The Guardians having satisfied themselves that the pauper belonged to this Union. It is resolved that he be taken to without orders of removal. [Page 15]

5 January 1874. Edward **Wilkinson** formerly an inmate of the Workhouse was bound apprentice to George **Smith** (Baker of Holbeach) for a period of four years – the premium £12. M Smith to allow the boy twopence per week for the first two years three pence per week during the next year and fourpence per week during the last year. [Page 18]

19 January 1874. **Panks** Thomas reported to have been removed to Freebridge Lynn Union. [Page 19]

19 January 1874. **Fysh** Anthy. Resolved that the Contract made between him and the Guardians to be cancelled see page 15. [Page 19]

19 January 1874. **Smith** M^r Tailor Spalding – S. W. **Gilbert** a youth bound apprentice to M^r Smith complains his master does not find him work also that M^r Smith neither finds clothes or pocket money. Resolved that M^r Smith be written to on the subject. [Page 19]

19 January 1874. Lunacy. It was reported to the Board that James **Parsons** had been sent to the County Asylum. [Page 19]

2 February 1874. It was reported that James **Parsons** had been removed from the parish of Holbeach to the County Lunatic Asylum at Bracebridge. [Page 21]

2 February 1874. **Woodrow** Eliz^th Ann has been discharged from the County Asylum at Bracebridge. [Page 21]

2 February 1874. **Hicks** William. Ordered that James Hicks of Sutton Crosses be called upon to contribute 2/- weekly towards the maintenance of his father William Hicks. [Page 21]

2 February 1874. **Bett** Louisa. Mr **Bush** of Long Sutton complained by letter of the dishonest habits of this girl who was sent from the Union Workhouse into M^r Bush's service. It is resolved that R. O. **Winfrey** investigate the matter. [Page 22]

16 February 1874. **Shore** John. Tydd. A letter from the Local Government Board (N^o 9402A dated 13^th February 1874) accompanied by a copy of a letter purporting to be written by John **Shaw** of Tydd S^t Mary in which he stated he had applied to R O **Winfrey** for relief but without avail and asking the Local Government Board to order that relief be given him. Resolved that the Local Government Board be informed that this Board have fully investigated the case and are fully satisfied with their former decision and Shore being present he was offered the house. [Page 24]

16 February 1874. **Bush** John & **Bett** Louisa. Ordered that application be made to John Bush of Long Sutton for 7/3 the balance of wages due to Louisa Bett now a pauper inmate. [Page 24]

16 February 1874. **Peach** Emma Club foot Instrument to be provided under the direction of M^r **Harper**. [Page 24]

16 February 1874. **Woodward** W^m Children – W^m aged 11 Emma Jane aged 9 and Sarah Ann aged 7 years the children of the late William Woodward of Sutton Saint Eds – having applied through their Uncle for relief and the children being removable. It is ordered that enquiries be made as to their settlement and that orders of removal be taken out. [Page 24]

2 March 1874. Mr **Bycroft** thatcher of Whaplode brought William **Wignal** (the boy whom he took from the Workhouse) and complained he was idle and impudent and would not work. The boy was examined apart from the Master when he stated he lived well – slept well and had no fault to find. M^r Bycroft was asked whether he would take the boy and give him another trial. [Page 26]

2 March 1874. M^r **Waterman** the Overseer for the parish of Fleet having given an order to D^r **Harper** the Medical Officer for Fleet to attend upon Elizabeth **Franks** during her confinement contrary to the consolidated order the case not being of a sudden and urgent necessity and having been refused at the last meeting of the Guardians. Ordered that the Clerk inform D^r Harper that this Board will not be responsible for any fee in the above case and that M^r Waterman be informed of the decision of this Board. [Page 27]

16 March 1874. **Rowtham** apply to son for relief. [Page 31]

30 March 1874. Henry **Green** to go on trial one month to M^r **Holland**. [Page 34]

30 March 1874. Ordered that M^r **Roughton** of Moulton be requested to pay 4/- weekly towards the maintenance of his father. [Page 34]

13 April 1874. **Chiltern** Sarah, Easington Union. The Clerk reported he had written to the Clerk of the Easington Union and there appearing to be an error of the Birth residence and settlement of the pauper and that he had obtained further information. Ordered that the Clerk write again giving the information obtained. [Page 38]

13 April 1874. **Ringham** Robert appeared before the Board with reference to contributing towards the maintenance of his son who is now in the Lincoln County Asylum he agreed to pay 2/6 weekly and the Guardians agreed to accept the same. [Page 39]

27 April 1874. Ordered that a Warrant be obtained for the apprehension of Sarah **Helstrup** for deserting her child. [Page 43]

27 April 1874. **Whiley** John. A letter dated the 16^th & 24^th of April from the Lynn Union stating that John Whiley was at the present time in the Lynn Union Workhouse also asking this Board to repay

the maintenance. Resolved that the pauper be accepted and the relief repaid in the usual way. [Page 43]

27 April 1874. **Waltham** William Spalding Union. Resolved that this pauper be allowed 3/- weekly and that the Guardians of the Spalding Union be asked to pay the same on behalf of this Union (aged 80). [Page 43]

11 May 1874. M^rs **Plowright** of Pinchbeck having taken out of the workhouse two of **Rudkins** children appeared before the Board and stated she had obtained situations for the children. It is resolved that clothing be allowed to each child of the value of £1-15.0 Sarah to reside at M^r James **Waring** Pinchbeck £3 wages and Elizabeth to reside with M^r John **Remington** wages £2.12.0. [Page 46]

11 May 1874. **Wright** Edward. Medical Officer **Haines** recommends that Edward Wright be sent to the Convalescent home at Hunstanton. Resolved that he be sent and the Chairman signed the recommendation. [Page 46]

25 May 1874. **Marshall** R O had given orders for Cod Liver Oil to Jane **Smith** and which oil was not entered in D^r **Harpers** Medical report. Resolved that M^r Harpers attention be called to the omission and that he be requested to enter the same on the Report. [Page 48]

8 June 1874. Ordered that Susan **Wignall** have an Outfit of the value of £2-10-0. [Page 50]

8 June 1874. Sarah Ann **Parr** a Singlewoman having deserted her child Elizabeth Ann Parr by leaving the same with M^rs **Christopher** of Lutton and the child having now become chargeable It is ordered that R O **Winfrey** cause the woman to be apprehended and the usual reward £1.10 given for her apprehension. [Page 50]

8 June 1874. **Haines** A H having ommitted to enter in his Medical report book the wine recommended by him to be given to John **Barrat** Ordered that M^r Haines attention be called thereto and that he be requested to enter the same. [Page 51]

8 June 1874. Ordered that [*blank*] **Jessop** of Long Sutton on the recommendation of M^r A. B. **Ewen** be sent to Guys Hospital for Cataract. [Page 51]

8 June 1874. Ordered that the Sheffield Union be applied to asking them to relieve Joseph **Jackson** aged 68 residing with Joseph Jackson [*blank*] 4/- weekly until further notice. [Page 51]

22 June 1874. **Day** Emily aged 27 years. It being reported to this Board that the mother of this pauper Harriet Day W^d resides at Wainfleet Port office that she has an interest in 60 acres of land in Sutton Saint James, Skegness and Frieston Ordered that the Collector apply to M^rs Day to pay for the maintenance of her daughter now in the Union Workhouse costing 4/- per week. [Page 52]

22 June 1874. The Master having reported that he had obtained a Warrant for the apprehension of John **Sporton** for deserting his children – approved. The Grandmother of the above children having stated she was about to remove the children from the Workhouse Resolved that the Master be authorized to withdraw the Warrant. [Page 52]

6 July 1874. **Sweeney** Hannah aged 22 years. D^r **Harper** having recommended that this pauper be sent to the Devonshire Hospital Resolved that on receiving the necessary form from the Hospital that she be sent there. [Page 57]

20 July 1874. Keziah **Rowe** aged 91 years residing with Thomas **Hubbert** of Dowsdate [*Dowsdale*] in the parish of Whaplode applied for relief. She stated the Wisbech Union had been allowing her 3/6 weekly and that the R. O. of that Union had informed her that in future the relief would be paid through this Union. Resolved that the Wisbech Union be informed this Board would pay the relief on their sanctioning the same. [Page 59]

20 July 1874. Radford Union. Lucretia **Holland** and family now residing in the neighbourhood of Radford it is ordered that Radford Union be informed thereof and the relief discontinued. [Page 59]

20 July 1874. **Day** Emily Sutton Saint James. The Medical Officer for the Tydd District having ordered this pauper Mutton and Wine from the 15^th June last to the present day and according to his Medical report he has not seen her since the time first mentioned. It is ordered that the Clerk write to M^r **Haines** and inform him the Guardians would be glad to receive any observations he may have to make in the matter. [Page 59]

3 August 1874. The Clerk reported that James **Parsons** has been removed from the County Asylum. [Page 61]

3 August 1874. The Guardians of the Wisbech Union reported they would allow Keziah **Rowe** 3/- weekly. [Page 61]

3 August 1874. The following orders were made

That Alice **Pesterfield** be proceeded against by R. O. **Winfrey** for the relief advanced to her son.

That **Hart** be apprehended for deserting his family. [Page 61]

17 August 1874. A letter from the Worksop Union was read relative to James Parsons **Palmer** the pauper Lunatic recently discharged from the County Asylum stating that he had again become unmanagle [*sic*] and asking for instructions to remove him to the County Asylum. Resolved that Instructions be given as requested. [Page 64]

17 August 1874. **Christmas** James an inmate in the Lincoln County Asylum died on the 15th August instant. [Page 64]

17 August 1874. **Hodgson** Martin. Ordered that the Clerk enquire into the Settlement of this pauper and the necessary authority be signed by the Chairman and the Seal of the Board affixed thereto. [Page 65]

14 September 1874. **Hodgson** and Wife. The Guardians of the Spalding Union having agreed to take these paupers provided they are legally removeable And Mr **Crowden** having sent a certificate in the following words "It is my opinion that Hodgson will be permanently affected. The chances are that he will never recoved [*sic*]" Resolved that inasmuch as Mr Crowdens Certificate is indefinite Mr J H **Spence** be employed at a cost of 10/6 to go to Sutton Saint Edmunds and examine the paupers. [Page 69]

14 September 1874. **Sweeney** Hannah. This pauper now at Buxton having staid the full time allowed by their rules for the subscription paid by this Union and the Medical officer having reported it would be better for her to continue three weeks longer at an expense of 30/- Resolved that a Cheque be sent for that sum to enable her to stay at Buxton. [Page 69]

14 September 1874. **Betts** Sarah from the parish of Long Sutton being pregnant. It is ordered that steps be taken to affiliate the child.

**Burrell** Jane Whaplode having an illegitimate child It is ordered that steps be taken to obtain repayment from the father of the child. [Page 72]

14 September 1874. **Brown** George aged 53 years. The Lynn Union have sent this paupers statement as to the cause of his becoming chargeable to that Union – viz to the effect following that he had been in this workhouse from 8 May 1873 to 31 August 1874 on that day he told the Master he wanted to get to Norwich and stated he wanted to go before the Board – he did not go before the Board but Mr **Hart** told him he had spoken to the Board The porter told Brown the Board had given the Master 2/- for him and the porter gave him the 2/- and told him it was to assist him on the road – Brown went to the Station had 4½ railway fare to Sutton where he remained from Monday to Saturday he then went to Lynn paid 1/2½ railway fare he had 1/- given to him at Long Sutton he went into the Lynn Vagrant Ward on Saturday and into the Infirmary on Sunday.

The Guardians having investigated the matter and find the application to the Board was for assistance to seek employment it was granted and the officers deny that they in any way knew he was going otherwise than to Long Sutton and other statements of the man are untrue. [Page 72]

14 September 1874. Dr **Harper** appeared before the Board and stated he had tried to reduce the dislocation of George **White**s shoulder and asked the Board to allow the patient to be sent to Saint Thomas Hospital London – application granted. [Page 72]

14 September 1874. The wife of John **Sakins** of Moulton applied to have her cousin Hannah **Green** to reside with her – the application was granted and clothing to the extent of 25/- allowed. [Page 72]

28 September 1874. The Clerk reported that he had received a letter from the Spalding Union agreeing to accept **Hodgson** and requesting this Board to relieve on their behalf. [Page 75]

28 September 1874. Ordered that the Clerk write to the Wisbech Union and that Board to relieve Mary **Lavett** aged 71 years residing at Walsoken with 3/- weekly and charge the same to this Union. [Page 75]

28 September 1874. Ordered that the Wisbech Union be asked to give 6d per week additional to Keziah **Rowe** aged 91 years. [Page 76]

12 October 1874. Resolved that the Wisbech Union be asked to relieve on behalf of this Union Wm **Aucock** aged 73 years with 3/- weekly also supply him with one pair of shoes. [page 81]

26 October 1874. Mr **Loverage** appeared before the Board and applied to have Elizabeth **Fletcher** as a Servant aged 13 years. Resolved that Fletcher go one months trial. [Page 83]

9 November 1874. **Foster** Benjamin – Resolved that this man be discharged work being offered him. [Page 85]

9 November 1874. Robert **Hallyfax** appeared before the Board as to contributing towards the maintenance of his daughter Ann now an inmate of the Workhouse when he stated he should decline to contribute anything. Resolved that an Authority be signed and the Seal of the Board affixed thereto authorizing R. O. **Marshall** to summons **Hallifax** to show cause why he refuses to contribute towards the maintenance of his daughter. [Page 86]

9 November 1874. Ordered that the Clerk write to Mr. **Haines** as to omitting Mary Ann **Barratt** from his report. [Page 86]

23 November 1874. Mr. **Loverage** appeared before the Board with reference to the hiring of Elizabeth **Fletcher** he offered to give £2.12.0 per annum and the girl being before the Board stated she was perfectly satisfied with her place. Resolved that the hiring be agreed to and clothing to the amount of £2.0.0 be allowed. [Page 88]

23 November 1874. **Manton** W$^m$ Gedney Marsh – M$^r$ **Ewen** reported that he had visited this pauper at his residence on Sunday the 22$^{nd}$ instant, and William Mantons wife being before the Board stated M$^r$ Ewen had not at any time been to their house. Ordered that M$^r$ Ewen be written to asking him to explain the matter. [Page 88]

7 December 1874. **Robinson** Ann an inmate of the Workhouse appeared before the Board and stated she had sworn her child to George **Hubbert** living with M$^r$ Joseph **Taylor** of Holbeach Fen. Ordered that application be made to the father for the amount awarded by the Magistrates. [Page 90]

7 December 1874. **Rudkin** Elizabeth. The Rev$^d$ E. L. **Bennett** produced a letter from the Rev. W. **Wayett** of Pinchbeck asking that Elizabeth Rudkin might be removed from the Lincoln County Asylum to her sisters at Pinchbeck whose husband is a labourer (a Mr **Plowright**) and stating as a reason for these steps being taken that her sister would treat her kindly and thus perhaps cause her to be restored. Resolved that the Clerk write to the Spalding Union asking their assent to this course being adopted and if so whether they would relieve Rudkin on behalf of this Union. Resolved that should the Spalding Board consent and agree to pay Rudkin out relief on behalf of this Board that Dr. **Palmer** be at once written to asking him if it would be any advantage to the woman and if so an authority would be at once sent for him to discharge her. [Page 92]

7 December 1874. That a Summons had been taken out against Robert **Halifax** for the maintenance of his daughter and that on the day of the hearing the infant died and the daughter being about to leave the house the summons was withdrawn on Halifax agreeing to pay 2/- weekly. [Page 92]

7 December 1874. William **Tickler** of Whaplode shoemaker appeared before the Board and agreed to take Anthony **Johnson** an inmate of this House as an apprentice from the present time and serve a period of five years the premium to be £10 given in the usual way. Tickler agrees to pay Johnson one penny per week during the first two years 2$^d$ the third year 3$^d$ the 4$^{th}$ year and 4$^d$ the last year of the apprenticeship. [Page 92]

7 December 1874. Radford Union. Ordered that the Clerk write to the Radford Union enquiring whether they had agreed to relieve Lucretia **Holland** and her two children. [Page 93]

21 December 1874. **Holland** Lucretia. The Clerk of the Radford Union reported that this womans statement was not correct. She was informed that if the guardians ordered out relief that Board would repay as heretofore. [Page 95]

21 December 1874. **Rudkin** a Lunatic. D$^r$ **Palmer** reported that this Lunatic was quite unfit to be discharged from the Asylum – and the Clerk reported he had sent a copy of the letter to Mr **Wyate**. **Cardell** Write to D$^r$ Palmer as to this Lunatic. [Page 95]

18 January 1875. **Stevenson** Ann. Mr **Arthburthnot** having sent this pauper with a letter from the Bourn Union to him as to granting out relief, the pauper states she is 34 years of age has two children earns 13/- weekly and has a house rent free. She washes for M$^r$ Arthburthnot. She says it costs her 4/- for coals 3/- for soap. Resolved that this statement be sent to the Bourn Union and should they deem it necessary to give relief this Board will administer it on their giving the usual undertaking to repay the same. [Page 100A]

1 February 1875. Ordered that the Clerk write and ask the Guardians of the Spalding Union to relieve on behalf of this Union William **Tingle** and wife with 3/- weekly. [Page 102]

15 February 1875. Resolved that Ann **Hotchin** aged 9 years and John Hotchin aged 7 years (children of Widow Hotchin) now residing at Nᵒ 4 Red Lion Court with William Hotchin be relieved with 2/- weekly. [Page 107]

15 February 1875. Mʳ **Loverage** Draper of Holbeach appeared before the Board and stated he was about to leave Holbeach and wished to transfer Elizabeth **Fletcher** from his house to Mʳ **Hackney** Grocer. Resolved that his wish be granted. [Page 107]

15 February 1875. **Aucock** William Wisbech Union. Resolved that the Wisbech Union be authorized to relieve this pauper with 1/- additional weekly as recommended in their letter of the 20 ult. [Page 108]

1 March 1875. Mʳ Philip **Anderson** of Gedney Dike applied to take Mary **May** a pauper inmate as a domestic servant Resolved that Mʳ Anderson be allowed to take Mary May and that she be allowed clothing to the amount of 40/-. [Page 112]

29 March 1875. Resolved that Susan **Johnson** aged 14 years from Long Sutton enter the service of Mʳ Samuel **Wilkinson** of Fleet Fen – the wages to be at the rate of £3 per annum and the service to continue to the usual May hirings in 1876 also that £3 be allowed for clothing.
Resolved that Elizabeth **Woodrow** go to Mrs **Williamson**s for one month on trial. [Page 117]

29 March 1875. It was reported to the Board by the Master that Wᵐ **Faulkener** was taken before Mr **Barker** J. P. for Vagrancy and such statement the following letter was ordered to be sent to Mr Barker:

It was reported to the Guardians on Monday last the 29ᵗʰ ultimo that William **Faulkner** lately an inmate of this Union Workhouse was brought before you in your magisterial capacity under the Vagrancy Act for sleeping in an outhouse and the fact was clearly proved by the police, And it was further reported you discharged the prisoner upon the condition that he became an inmate of the Union Workhouse. The Board direct me to observe that they have not the slightest wish to offer one word of dictation to you in your magisterial capacity but I am directed to suggest to you as mbr of this Board the difficulties which must necessarily attend their ministerial duties if they are not supported by the justices, The object of the Board is to insist that the man earns his own living which if temperate he is fully able to do. I trust as does the Board you will not consider this letter as in the slightest degree wanting in politeness or offensive. [Page 117]

12 April 1875. Resolved that Edward **Chettle** a pauper inmate aged 15 years be allowed to enter the service of Mʳ Wᵐ **Pitts** and that the wages be £3 from the present time to the 13ᵗʰ day of May 1876 and that Clothing be allowed to the same amount. [Page 121]

12 April 1875. Ordered that the Medical Officer **Vise** be requested to report upon the condition of William **Tingle** by the next Board day. [Page 121]

12 April 1875. Mʳ Mowbray **Chapman** applied to have Maud **Chettle** for a Servant. Resolved that Chettle go to Mʳ Chapman one month on trial. [Page 121]

26 April 1875. Ordered that an Authority be signed authorising the Clerk to Summon George **Westmorland** for the arrears of maintenance of his father. [Page 126]

26 April 1875. Robert **Brown** agrees to pay 4/- weekly towards the maintenance of his wife. [Page 127]

26 April 1875. Ordered that steps be taken to get the child of Caroline **Gibbens** affiliated. [Page 127]

26 April 1875. Mr **Caparn** agreed to take Hy **Johnson** one month on trial the terms to be afterwards arranged. [Page 127]

26 April 1875. That the Friendly Society of Sutton Bridge be written to as to the payment of 2/6 weekly towards the maintenance of J. B. **Triffitt**. [Page 127]

26 April 1875. That Caroline **Woodrow** be allowed clothing to the amount of £2.13.0 on her entering Mʳ **Williamson**s service and the wages to the 13ᵗʰ May 1876 be the same amount. [Page 127]

10 May 1875. The attention of the Board having been called by the Master to a paragraph in the paper (Lincolnshire Chronicle) that Frederick **Smith** had been taken before the Magistrates at Lincoln and being destitute Mʳ **Rudgard** had given him money to pay his Railway fare to Long Sutton. It is ordered that enquiries be made as to the circumstances under which Frederick Smith was sent from Lincoln to Long Sutton. [Page 130]

24 May 1875. A letter from the Rev$^d$ John **Young** with reference to the payment of Mrs **Lavett**s relief was read. Resolved on the Wisbech Union pay the relief this Board will repay the Wisbech Union. [Page 132]

24 May 1875. **Caparn** M$^{rs}$ having written stating they were quite willing to take the Boy Henry **Johnson** as a Servant. Ordered that the Master arrange with M$^{rs}$ Caparn and that this Board will allow £3.0.0 for Clothing and wages are to be three pounds. [Page 132]

24 May 1875. The master reported that the Nurse had left the patients in the infirmary without a proper officer to attend them and against the consent of the Matron the nurse stated she did so at the request of the Rev$^d$ W. **James** to take Hannah **Sweeney** out of the Workhouse. Ordered that M$^r$ James be written to requesting him not to induce officers to break the discipline of the house and the nurse requested to obey the orders of the Matron according to the orders of the Local Gov$^t$ Board. [Page 132]

24 May 1875. The Master also reported he had reason to believe Brandy was brought into the house by Visitors to the man **Tomlinson** in the sick ward and the male nurse stated he kept it under his Bed the nurse (**Rush**) stated she found a bottle under the bed and took it away and she drank it with the consent of the many friends. [Page 132]

24 May 1875. Chapman **Mowbray** applied for clothing for Maud **Chettle** whom he took out of the House as a Servant. Resolved that the application be granted the wages to be 50/- and clothing of the same amount. [Page 133]

24 May 1875. **Hackney** H. A. of Gedney Drove End having written stating he had undertaken to bring up John **Hotchin** without relief it is ordered that the Boston Union be written to requesting them to discontinue the relief. [Page 133]

7 June 1875. M$^r$ **Caparn**s letter to M$^r$ **Francklin** was read with reference to the boy **Johnson** whom he had taken into his Service. M$^r$ Caparn declines to pay wages but will find all clothing. Ordered that M$^r$ Caparn be informed that this Board cannot depart from their regular rule. [Page 134]

7 June 1875. **Sweeney** Hannah. The Rev$^d$ E. L. **Bennett** brought to this Board the letter written by the Clerk to the Rev$^d$ **James** of Fleet also a private letter written to him by M$^r$ James both of which he read to the Board (and took them away with him). Mr Bennett commented upon the Clerks letter and proposed that the Clerks letter to Mr James and Mr James letter to M$^r$ Bennett having been read the Board regrets the terms in which the one addressed to M$^r$ James was couched and which they had not previously had read to them. Seconded by Mr **Blower**. Mr **Carbutt** proposed that no such proposition be carried. Seconded by Mr **Wilkinson**. The amendment was put to the Meeting when there appeared to be 10 for the amendment and three against it. The Chairman not voting – The amendment was declared carried. [Page 134]

21 June 1875. A letter from the Spalding Union was read asking this Board to take Joseph **Gull** aged 75 years without orders of removal and asking this Board to allow that Union to pay him 3/6 weekly on behalf of this Union. Ordered that enquiries be made as to Gulls removability and should it be found that Gull is removeable that the relief be granted.[Page 136]

21 June 1875. A letter No 38325 B dated 14$^{th}$ June 1875 from the Local Government Board, accompanied by a copy of a letter addressed to them by the Rev W. K. **James**, a copy of a letter sent by the Clerk of this Board to Mr James also a copy of a letter sent by Mr James to the Rev$^d$ E. L. **Bennett** – The Local Government boards letter contained request to be furnished with any observations the Guardians might wish to offer on the Subject. Ordered that the Clerk send a copy of the Masters report as follows:

May 24$^{th}$ 1875. I beg to report that on May the 15$^{th}$ the nurse left the house without leave, deceived the Matron with reference to the discharge of **Sweeney** an inmate and used improper language to the Matron. Also send a copy of the resolution thereon and a copy of the last resolution. [Page 138]

21 June 1875. From the Medical report for the Long Sutton District it appeared that Susan **Holmes** had not been visited between the 1$^{st}$ of May and the 30$^{th}$ May. Ordered that the Clerk write to the Medical officers stating that it does not appear to the Board that the visits of the Medical officers to the paupers are so numerous as the cases require particularly in the Long Sutton District. [Page 138]

21 June 1875. **Head** Catharine aged 80 years residing at Hull and being a non resident pauper sent a letter asking for an increase of relief. Ordered that she be allowed 3/6 weekly should the Guardians of the Sculcoates Union deem that amount necessary. [Page 138]

21 June 1875. Resolved that J. W. **Hart** the Master of the Union Workhouse summon John Tobias **Parsons** to show cause why he neglects to maintain Emma his wife and Florence their child now inmates of the workhouse and chargeable to the Union. [Page 141]

19 July 1875. Ordered that Robert **Rowden** aged 55 on Holbeach Bank and who is suffering from Rheumatism be sent to Buxton. [Page 143]

16 August 1875. **Baxter** Cason aged 62 years. A letter dated 7th instant from the West Ham Union was read stating this man was now in their union workhouse and that he had left this Union in March last – and asking this Board to take him without orders of removal. Resolved that inasmuch as he belongs to this Union that an order be sent for his admission into this Workhouse. [Page 147]

16 August 1875. **Savage** Emma aged 33 years having on the 5th July 1875 been adjudicated a Lunatic and removed by the Guardians of the city of London Union to the County Asylum at Kent and the said Guardians having obtained an order for the costs of her removal to the County Asylum at Stone and for her removal and maintenance to the 27th July and for her future maintenance there the Grounds of Settlement relied upon are that she is the daughter of Thomas and Louisa **Worth** – that she hired a house in Holbeach of £10 and upwards paid rates and taxes and resided therein 40 nights – that she was the W[o] of W Savage and that he had hired land in Whaplode of more than £10 rental and had paid the rates and taxes and resided therein 40 nights where he died that the said Thomas Worth for the past 40 years and paid the rent of £10 & upwards and served the office of Guardians for the past 34 years. From the above facts it is resolved not to appeal against the orders and it was ordered that steps be taken to cause her removal to the County Asylum at Bracebridge – Mr Worth being present stated all the expenses would be paid. [Page 147]

30 August 1875. Ordered that the Whittlesea Union be written to asking them to relieve on behalf of this Union Sarah **Birch** 75 years of age and chargeable to this Union and who intends residing with Mr **Smith** Carpenter Whitmore street Whittlesea with [blank]. [Page 150]

27 September 1875. A letter from the Whittlesey Board of Guardians requesting to have a Guarantee for funeral and other expences for W[o] **Birch** should she die. Ordered that the usual guarantee be given. [Page 156]

27 September 1875. Mr John **Smith** of Whaplode Saddler applies to have George **Wade** (aged 13 years) apprenticed to him. Resolved that Wade go one month on trial to M[r] Smith. [Page 156]

27 September 1875. Grimsby Fishery. M[r] Matthew **Porter** wrote enquiring whether any Boy in the workhouse were desirous of the Sea Service. John **Hall** an orphan aged 13 years applied to go. Resolved that M[r] Porter be informed thereof. [Page 156]

27 September 1875. **Stevens** W[m]. Orders of Removal were read from Saint Pancras Union whereby the Guardians of that Union intend to remove William Stevens to this Union. Resolved the orders be not appealed against. [Page 156]

11 October 1875. **May** Mary & **Anderson** Philip E. Resolved Mr Anderson be paid for the Clothing supplied to May after deducting the amount of Wages due to her and the clothing being returned to the Guardians. [Page 162]

11 October 1875. **Took** Susan and her three children having become chargeable to this union through the desertion by her husband. It is resolved that the usual reward be paid for his apprehension and that the master obtain a warrant for his apprehension and the usual authority be signed by the chairman. [Page 162]

11 October 1875. Simon **Farrow** of Whaplode Drove Saddler having applied to have Mary **May** as a domestic Servant and take her on trial – granted. [Page 162]

11 October 1875. M[r] W **Jackson** Overseer of Gedney Hill applied to have F **Pape** aged 13 years as a Servant – granted on trial. [Page 162]

25 October 1875. **James** Rev[d] W H. A letter N[o] 60670B dated 15th October 1875 from the Local Government Board was read – as to **Sweeney** the Board stated they had received a letter from M[r] James stating if the nurse informed the Matron that she left the Workhouse at his request to take Hannah Sweeney out of the Workhouse she stated that which was in every respect contrary to the fact; that every thing was done in the presence of the Master and he believed at the time the Master approved and sanctioned Sweeney's being removed, that he was quite ignorant of any breach of discipline on the part of the house or that any regulation had been infringed. The Local Government Board trust that this explanation will remove the unfavourable impression which the

Guardians appear to have had as regards the proceedings of Mr James in the case referred to. Ordered that Mr James be furnished with a copy of this letter. [Page 165]

25 October 1875. Mr **Smith** of Moulton attended before the Board with reference to George **Wade** being bound apprentice to him. Mr Smith declined to take him without a premium alth: he would be partly employed in agriculture. Mr **Blower** proposed That the boy be not apprenticed. Seconded by Mr **West** and Unanimously carried. [Page 165]

8 November 1875. A letter from the Rev Walter **James** was read stating he had previously received a copy of the Local Government Boards Letter but did not know upon what grounds the guardians had honoured him with a copy – and requesting to know if the "unfavourable impression which the Guardians appear to have had" is removed. No reply. [Page 167]

8 November 1875. **Wade** [*blank*] of Tydd Saint Mary applied to this Board with reference to his son living with Mr **Smith** of Moulton, he required Clothing for the Boy, he did not know the terms of the hiring – the Guardians requested Wade to make further enquiries and apply again. [Page 167]

8 November 1875. Mr **Worth** being desirous of getting his wife removed from the London Asylum where now as to the County Asylum in consequence of great expense and he having to maintain his daughter in the County Asylum Resolved that the removal take place on Mr Worth signing the usual undertaking to repay the Asylum charges. [Page 168]

22 November 1875. Ordered that the Clerk write to the Lynn Union and inform that Union informing them that Sarah **Blackster** had left this Union and was no longer relieved on their behalf. [Page 170]

6 December 1875. Ordered that Frederick **Pape** formerly in this Union Workhouse but now residing with Mrs **Deippe** 54½ Long acre London be bound apprentice to learn the trade of a butcher term 4 years – to have a suitable outfit and the usual notices be given to the Guardians of the Union in which he resides. [Page 173]

3 January 1876. **Boatwright** a Servant. Mr **Wright** in whose service this Girl is wrote to state that her behaviour was such that he could not keep her in his house. Ordered that the Girl return to the Workhouse. [Page 179]

17 January 1876. The Collector was ordered to apply for Charles **Jackson**'s pension towards his maintenance in the House. [Page 181]

17 January 1876. Esther **Edgeley** aged 31 applied on behalf of herself and Charles aged 6 and Susan 2 that she should be allowed 3/- per week to be paid to her at George **Robinsons** East Leake Nr Loughborough. The application was granted subject to the usual enquiries being satisfactory. [Page 182]

31 January 1876. To write to the Authorities at Liverpool informing them that Esther **Walker** had become permanently disabled and chargeable to this Union. [Page 185]

31 January 1876. To write in reply that this Union would not apprentice Frederick **Pape** and that the Board would adhere to the regulations made at the time the boy was sent. [Page 185]

14 February 1876. Ordered that enquiries be made as to the Settlement of Mary **George** wife of Samuel George her husband came from Hemington near Oundle. [Page 186]

14 February 1876. The Committee reported that they were informed that William **Goodwin** does not pay to the support of his Bastard child by Sarah **Bennett**. [Page 186]

28 February 1876. The Clerk was directed to summons William **Goodwin** of Long Sutton Rat-catcher to contribute towards the maintenance of Sarah **Bennett**'s bastardy child of whom he is the reputed Father. [Page 187]

28 February 1876. The Clerk was to write to Mrs Mary **Mellors** and inform her that the amount of Mrs **King**'s relief would no longer be paid to her direct the Guardians considering that Mrs King's allowance should be paid through the proper officers of the Union in which she resides. [Page 187]

28 February 1876. Ordered that the Master purchase an Elastic Stocking **Mair** Son & Compy for Elizabeth **Younghusband**. [Page 187]

13 March 1876. The Workhouse Master reported that the Inspector for this District recommends that the Boy Mills **Brace** who is an idiot in this workhouse should be sent to the Eastern Counties Idiot Asylum Colchester. The Clerk was directed to write to the Superintendent and ask what the cost of the Boy's maintenance would be. [Page 190]

13 March 1876. The Clerk was directed to write to Mr **Worth** with reference to his ability to maintain Mrs **Worth** & Mrs **Savage** Lunatics in the County Asylum. [Page 190]

13 March 1876. The Chairman signed the usual Authority for a summons against William **Goodwin** for neglecting to contribute towards the maintenance of Sarah **Bennet**'s bastard child and the Seal of the Board was affixed thereto. [Page 190]

27 March 1876. D<sup>r</sup> **Harper** reported a case of an apprentice named **Barker** with Scarlet fever who had been sent home to Holbeach Hurn while suffering from Scarlet fever. Ordered that the Clerk give notice thereof to the Holbeach Local Board and request them to take steps to punish the Master. [Page 193]

27 March 1876. The Clerk was directed to write to the Lincoln Aslylum Authorities and to inform them that this Board are of opinion that M<sup>rs</sup> **Savage** and M<sup>rs</sup> **Worth** should not be maintained as Pauper Lunatics in the Asylum. [Page 193]

27 March 1876. The Clerk was also directed to write to the Guardians of Spalding Union and inform them that this Board have given instructions that if **Winkley** applies at this Workhouse he shall be admitted in due course. [Page 193]

27 March 1876. Ordered that the Clerk write to the Guardians of Wisbech Union and inform them that Mary **Sketchen** is dead. [Page 193]

27 March 1876. The Clerk was directed to write to M<sup>rs</sup> Mary **Mellor** and to inform her that the Clapham and Wandsworth Board of Guardians having refused to undertake the payment of the relief to M<sup>rs</sup> **King** she must return to her own parish as no further payments will be made except through the Relieving Officer of this Union. [Page 193]

10 April 1876. A letter from the Superintendent of the Lincoln County Asylum was read. The Clerk was directed to send a reply and to state that this Board no longer intend to pay for the maintenance of Louisa **Worth** a pauper Lunatic in the asylum but with regard to Emma **Savage** the Board are satisfied with the present arrangement and they will continue to pay as heretofore. [Page 199]

10 April 1876. The Clerk was directed to take the necessary steps for the affiliation of Mary **Joyce**'s child. [Page 199]

10 April 1876. Ordered that the Clerk write to M<sup>r</sup> **Chapman** and inform him that this Board are willing to let him have the child **Dolton** and to give her an outfit upon the condition that he pay her wages at the rate of one shilling per week. [Page 199]

24 April 1876. The Clerk was directed to report the death of Ann **Martin** a non-settled Pauper of Sutton Bridge to the Guardians of the Wisbech Union. [Page 202]

8 May 1876. The Clerk was directed to write to the Guardians of Wisbech Union and to request them to accept a Pauper named Lydia **Butcher** residing in this Union workhouse, aged 17 years, without an order of Removal. [Page 204]

22 May 1876. Ordered that the Clerk apply to the Committee of Managers of Devonshire Hospital Buxton for an Order of Admission into their hospital for a poor woman named Eliza **Jacobs** aged 34 years residing in the district of M<sup>r</sup> **Marshall** the Relieving Officer of this Union. [Page 206]

22 May 1876. The Clerk was directed to write to M<sup>r</sup> **Millns**, the Collector of the Guardians, and to request him to collect from the Forresters Club, Holbeach, the relief advanced to Thomas **Smith**, residing in this Union Workhouse being a member of that Club. [Page 206]

22 May 1876. Ordered that the Clerk write to the Guardians of Spalding Union and request them to pay Rebecca **Brittain**, aged 69, a Pauper belonging to this Union 3/- weekly and charge it to the account of this Union. [Page 206]

22 May 1876. The Clerk was directed to write to the Guardians of Boston Union and to request them to pay to W **Hotchen** the Grandfather of the child **Sketchin** 2/- weekly and to direct their Relieving Officer to ascertain the age and christian name of the child. [Page 206]

22 May 1876. A letter from M<sup>r</sup> **Starbuck**, Photographer, of Long Sutton, was read in which he agrees to take the child **Bennett** for a period of 12 months at a 1/- per week wages. Ordered that the Clerk prepares the usual Contract. [Page 206]

22 May 1876. Ordered that Esther **Boatwright** on the recommendation of M<sup>r</sup> **Wilkinson** go to M<sup>r</sup> **Cave** of Fleet Fen, for a month on Trial. [Page 206]

22 May 1876. The Clerk was directed to enforce the Order made upon William **Goodwin** for the maintenance of Sarah **Bennet**'s bastard child. [Page 206]

# EXTRACTS FROM THE HOLBEACH UNION WORKHOUSE MINUTES
## PL8/102/20 1873 - 1876

22 May 1876. A letter from the Guardians of Wisbeach Union was read in which they agreed to accept a pauper named Lydia **Butcher** who resides in this Union Workhouse aged 17 years without an order of removal. [Page 207]

22 May 1876. A letter from the Guardians of Derby Union was read in which they request the Guardians of this Union to accept a pauper named George **Reed** without an Order of Removal. Ordered that the Clerk make the usual enquiries before accepting the pauper. [Page 207]

1 June 1876. The Clerk informed the Board that he had caused enquiries to be made respecting the Settlement of George **Reed** whom the Guardians of Derby Union request this Board to accept without an Order of removal. Reed's settlement from the enquiries made appears to be Tydd S$^t$ Mary in this Union. Ordered that the Pauper be accepted and that the Clerk give Notice thereof to Derby Union. [Page 208]

1 June 1876. Letter from the Authorities of the Devonshire Hospital Buxton was read in which they stated that a vacancy would occur in their Institution for a Patient on the 12$^{th}$ June inst. Ordered that Eliza **Jacobs** of Holbeach be removed to the Hospital on that day. [Page 208]

1 June 1876. Ordered that the Clerk write to Edwin **Cook** and Hezekiah Cook both of Gedney Hill calling on them to contribute towards the maintenance of their Father who is in receipt of relief from this Union (Father's name John Cook). [Page 209]

15 June 1876. Letter from the Wandsworth and Clapham Union Guardians enclosing a letter from M$^{rs}$ Mary **Mellor** was read in which she asks for relief for M$^{rs}$ **King** a Non-resident-Pauper who was struck off the relief list by Order of this Board for a few weeks since. Ordered that the Clerk write to the Wandsworth Guardians and inform them that this Board are willing to grant such relief to M$^{rs}$ King through the officers of Wandsworth Union as the Wandsworth & Clapham Guardians think proper. [Page 210]

15 June 1876. The Clerk was directed to write to the Commanding Officer of the Royal Militia, Grantham, and to request him to cause William **Dunthorpe** a Soldier to contribute towards the maintenance of his wife & 4 children who are in receipt of relief from this Union. [Page 210]

29 June 1876. Letter from the Guardians of Beverley Union was read stating that Catherine **Head** has come from Hull Union to their Union and has applied to their Board for Non-Residential Relief. Ordered that the Clerk reply thereto and inform them that they may advance 3/6 weekly to the above named Pauper belonging to this Union. [Page 2]

29 June 1876. Letter from the Commanding Officer of the Royal South Lincolnshire Militia was received in which he states that the soldier William **Dunthorpe** has consented to allow sixpence a day of his pay to be paid towards the maintenance of his wife & 4 children who are receiving relief from this Union. [Page 2]

29 June 1876. Ordered that the Clerk write to Edwin **Cook** and Hezikiah Cook and request the former to pay 2/- weekly and the latter 1/6 weekly towards the maintenance of their father John Cook who is in this Union Workhouse. [Page 3]

29 June 1876. The Clerk was directed to write to James **Mumby** and George Mumby both of Long Sutton to contribute 2$^s$/5$^d$ each weekly towards the maintenance of their Father who also is in this Union Workhouse. [Page 3]

13 July 1876. Ordered that the Clerk give Messrs **Mumby** notice that they will be made to contribute if their Father comes into the house again. [Page 5]

13 July 1876. William **Cardwell** in Lincoln County Asylum belongs to Whaplode Benefit Society Ordered that the Society be applied to the relief due to him. [Page 5]

13 July 1876. Ordered that D$^r$ **Harpers** attention be called to the operation on Mary **Downham** by Mr Russell Harper without any assistance that M$^r$ **Carter** was present. [Page 5]

13 July 1876. **Marshall** – Removing Eliz **Jacobs** from Devonshire Hosp          £2.5.6 [Page 5]

13 July 1876. Stephen **Gardiner** 12 years of age & Mr **Brewin** attended the Board and an agreement was ordered to be made as Servant 1/= a week and washing &c. from now to Mayday £2. for clothes & a Bible. [Page 5]

10 August 1876. Re Mrs **King**. Letter to Clapham Union that money was to be paid – Mr **Millns** must obtain payment from the School Board. [Page 8]

10 August 1876. That Susanna **Aldred** have her son's clothes on the recommendation of the Master. [Page 8]

24 August 1876. Ordered that a letter be written to the Guardians of the Spalding Union in reply that Joseph **Jones** whose settlement is Gedney Hill would be admitted into the Workhouse. [Page 9]

24 August 1876. Ordered that a letter be written to M$^r$ **Millns** directing him to apply for a warrant against **Goodwin** if he has not paid towards the maintenance of Sarah **Bennett**s bastard child. [Page 9]

24 August 1876. **Braybrook** Bricklayer of Whaplode applied that **Wilson** should be apprenticed to him for 7 years - application refused. [Page 9]

7 September 1876. Ordered that a Warrant be issued against W$^m$ **Goodwin** as often as he shall be in arrear in his payment for 4 weeks. [Page 11]

21 September 1876. **Smith** – Spalding – **Gilbert**s Clothing          £1.10.0  [Page 14]

21 September 1876. Ordered that the Clerk take the necessary proceedings to affiliate Mary Louisa **Groom**s Bastard Child. [Page 14]

21 September 1876. That he write to M$^r$ **Vise** requesting him to report upon the case of John **Cordell** at Whaplode. [Page 14]

21 September 1876. That he write as soon as John **Boardman** goes to Northampton to the Northampton Union requesting them to pay 3/6 a week and charge the same to non settled $^a$/c. [*in pencil*] John Boardman at M$^r$ Davis's 26 Grafton St Nthampton. [Page 14]

19 October 1876. Ordered that the cost of Conveying Geo: **Money** to a London Hospital on the recommendation of Medical Officer be paid. [Page 21]

2 November 1876. Ordered that a Letter be written to Horncastle Union enquiring if the Board should pay Sarah **Green** now residing at Lutton aged 80 – 3/- a week. [Page 22]

16 November 1876. Ordered that the Clerk write to the Docking Union to inform them that Sarah **Riches** & her two children had become chargeable to this Union & to request them to repay the Guardians the money expended. [Page 24]

16 November 1876. Ordered that the Clerk write to Spalding Union requesting them to pay Hannah **Pepper** aged 18 3/- a week. [Page 24]

16 November 1876. Ordered that the Clerk write to the Collector to collect the Lunacy a/cs viz Louisa **Worth**, Emma **Savage**, William **Hicks** and Sarah **Richards**. [Page 24]

30 November 1876. Ordered that a Summons be issued against W$^m$ **Clark** horse-dealer living at Wisbech S$^t$ Peter for leaving his wife & child chargeable to the Union. [Page 26]

30 November 1876. Ordered that a letter be written to [*blank*] **Congreve** of Sutton Bridge Long Sutton requesting payment towards the maintenance of his Mother Mary Ann Congreve. [Page 26]

30 November 1876. Robin **Brown** attended and the Board consented to his payments being reduced to 1/- per week from Michaelmas last. [Page 26]

14 December 1876. The Clerk reported that W$^m$ **Clarke** had paid the costs incurred in allowing his wife & child to become chargeable to the Union & had been ordered by the Magistrates to pay 3/6 a week. [Page 27]

14 December 1876. The Board allowed Abraham **Watty** [*Watte*] & wife 4/- a week from today & ordered the money to be repaid by their sons viz [Page 27]

| | | |
|---|---|---|
| John Watty | Lincoln | on Staff of Lincolnshire Chronicle |
| Abraham Watty | Holbeach | Foreman of Brickyard |
| Levi Watty 3 chn | ditto | Labourer to A Watty |
| Jesse Watty | Lincoln | Police Lincoln City Force |

14 December 1876. Ordered that a letter be written to **Jibb** of Lutton Garnsgate requiring repayment towards the maintenance of his Mother. [Page 28]

14 December 1876. Ordered that the Clerk sign an order for the admission of Widow **Congreve** & if she comes into the house her son must be summoned for not contributing to her maintenance. [Page 28]

14 December 1876. M$^{rs}$ **Smith** Baker applied that a boy **Wilson** now in the house should be apprenticed to her the Board referred the application. [Page 28]

14 December 1876. Ordered that the Clerk apply to the Horncastle Guardians for repayment of the funeral expenses &c of Widow **Green**. [Page 28]

28 December 1876. Ordered that the Clerk write to M$^r$ **Wilson** farmer Tydd St Mary for a contribution towards the maintenance of his wife in the Lunatic Asylum. [Page 29]

25 January 1877. Ordered that the necessary proceedings be taken to affiliate Elizabeth **Ball**'s Bastard Child. [Page 33]

8 February 1877. Ordered that the Clerk employ a Solicitor to prosecute in the case of **Balls** v Balls & in other similar cases in which he is unable to do it himself. [Page 35]

8 February 1877. Ordered that the Clerk make enquiries as to the whereabouts of [*blank*] **Bennett** whose wife Esther & two children Martha and John had become chargeable to the Union. [Page 35]

22 February 1877. Ordered that the Clerk take the necessary steps to affiliate Caroline **Child**'s bastard child. [Page 37]

8 March 1877. William **Hart** was brought by the Master before the Board to explain his conduct in absconding. After the School master had explained to the Board how it was the lad was enabled to run away. The Chairman informed the School Master that he must not leave the boys alone at any time & also reprimanded the lad & informed him he would be punished severely if anything of the kind occurred again. [Page 39]

8 March 1877. Ordered that Frederick **Pilgrim** be summoned for neglecting to maintain his child if he did not remove the child from the workhouse tomorrow. [Page 40]

22 March 1877. Ordered that the Clerk obtain an order for the removal of Susannah **Greetham** to the Peterborough Union. [Page 42]

22 March 1877. The Master reported that Charles **Dixon** a lad in the School had absconded in Workhouse Clothes while out walking with the School Master. The Schoolmaster was directed not to allow the boys to go out of his sight. [Page 42]

22 March 1877. The attention of the Board was called to a report in the Boston Guardian relative to Daniel **Pickett** an inmate of the infirmary stating that this man had been reported dead and that in consequence he had not been supplied with his dinner. After hearing the statement of the Master the nurse and attendant the Board came to the conclusion that there was no ground for the story and the Clerk was directed to write to the Editor enquiring who communicated the report. [Page 42]

22 March 1877. On the application of George **Taylor** leave was given for Thomas George **Rodyers** to go to him for a month on trial upon the usual terms. [Page 43]

5 April 1877. On the application of Emma **Parsons** an inmate the Clerk was directed to make enquiries & if the address of her husband could be obtained to take proceedings against the Husband for non maintenance of his wife. [Page 45]

5 April 1877. The Clerk was also directed to make enquiries into the cases of Sarah Ann **Line** & John **Coe** from Manchester. [Page 45]

5 April 1877. Ordered that the Collector apply to the **Cooks** of Gedney Hill for £1-8-6 funeral expenses of their father. [Page 45]

19 April 1877. Emily **Coley** a pauper inmate applied that a warrant should be issued against her husband who had deserted her. Ordered that the necessary proceedings be taken for his apprehension. [Page 51]

19 April 1877. Thomas **Mumby** applied that Esther **Boatwright** be allowed to enter his service for a year – application was however refused.[Page 51]

19 April 1877. Leave was given to James **Wilson** a pauper lad to go to Edw$^d$ **Bycroft** Thatcher Whaplode for a month on trial. [Page 51]

3 May 1877. Ordered that George **Taylor** apprenticed to Thomas George **Rogers** have clothes to the value of 52/- on the condition that his master pay him 1/- per week for a year. [Page 53]

3 May 1877. Ordered that Esther **Boatwright** be allowed to go to M$^r$ David **Oliver** of Fleet, on service. [Page 53]

17 May 1877. Ordered that the Guardians of the Spalding Union be requested to relieve Ann **Porter** aged 76 living with John **Trees** M$^r$ **Chambers** Farmer Moulton Chapel. [Page 54]

31 May 1877. M$^{rs}$ **Nunn** complained that when in the house the Medical Officer refused to give herself & children medicine. Order for the house. [Page 56]

31 May 1877. Ordered that the Clerk write to the Sons of Abraham **Watty** & wife threatening proceedings if they did not contribute to their parents expenses in the house. [Page 56]

31 May 1877. Ordered that James **Wilson** be apprenticed to Edward **Bycroft** Whaplode Thatcher & that he be allowed the usual grant of clothes. [Page 56]

14 June 1877. The Master reported that Ellen **Fenn** had gone for a month on Trial to M$^r$ **Jakes** Whaplode. [Page 58]

14 June 1877. Ordered that the Clerk write to the Clerk of Glanford Brigg Union empowering the Guardians to receive Sarah **Coe** aged 85 into the workhouse. [Page 58]

28 June 1877. Ordered that the Clerk write to **Wattys** children to inform them the Guardians on his request advanced him 6$^s$/- a week, on the understanding that his children should be called upon to repay the amount between them, and unless they entered into an Agreement with the Guardians before next Board Day, to pay such Relief, a Summons would be issued for such repayment. [Page 60]

28 June 1877. M$^r$ **Jakes** agreed to take **Fenn** as servant up to May-Day and pay her 1$^s$/- a week wages, and it was Ordered that a Sum of 40$^s$/- be allowed for her clothes. [Page 60]

28 June 1877. The Clerk was instructed to write to M$^r$ Jabez **Clifton** of Gedney in answer to his letter, and to inform him they could not accede to his request for providing clothes for **Clarke** a boy in his service. [Page 60]

12 July 1877. Ordered that George & Thomas **Mumby** be summoned to show cause why they should not contribute 2$^s$/- a week, towards their Fathers maintenance. [Page 62]

12 July 1877. Ordered that Abraham & Jesse **Watty** be summoned in like manner for neglecting to maintain their Father in pursuance of Notice duly given. [Page 62]

12 July 1877. The Clerk was instructed to write to M$^r$ **Garner** of Sutton Marsh to apply to him for £6.13.10 due to the Guardians as Representatives of George **Humphrey** being amount due for Labr. [Page 62]

12 July 1877. The Clerk was also instructed to write to Mrs **Kingston** of Lutton Marsh for £3, being amount left by George **Humphrey** in her hands. [Page 62]

25 July 1877. The Clerk was instructed to make enquiries respecting William **King** a Pauper who had become chargeable to the Holbeach Union, and who it appears had been a resident for some time past at Sibsey in the Boston Union, and to write to the Clerk of that Union, to send an Order for King's Admission into the Boston Union, without Justice's Order. [Page 64]

26 July 1877. J **Holmes** xps burying **Woodhouse** died in St Thomas' Hospital   £3.18.0 [Page 64]

9 August 1877. A letter was read from the Clerk of the Newport Pagnel Union stating that a Lunatic Pauper named John **Bloy** who it appeared formerly resided at Tydd S$^t$ Mary, and who had been in the Bracebridge Asylum for many years, was found wandering in that Union on the 30$^{th}$ July. He was apprehended by the Police there for exposing his person and had been sent to the Bucks County Asylum. The Guardians authorised the cost of the Paupers maintenance in such Asylum, to be charged against the Holbeach Union until steps were taken for his removal to the Bracebridge Asylum. [Page 66]

23 August 1877. An Extract from the Boston Guardian was read relative to M$^{rs}$ **Fenn** and her children, and inquiry was made of the Relieving Officer which satisfied the Guardians that M$^{rs}$ Fenn was acquainted with the Rules of the House, and that she was in the town from 4 o'clock in the afternoon, and so had ample opportunity of coming into the house before 9 o'clock. [Page 68]

23 August 1877. Ordered that if Benjamin **Sizee** remains in the house the Clerk do summons his son William Sizee for his maintenance. [Page 68]

6 September 1877. A letter from the Local Government Board enclosing copy of a letter addressed to them from a M$^r$ William **Banks** of Boston, to which was annexed an Extract from the "Boston Guardian" referring to the case of M$^{rs}$ **Fenn** & her children, to which attention had been given at the last Meeting of the Board, was read, asking for any observations the Guardians might make on the subject. The matter was again gone into. The Clerk was directed in reply to state the decision of the Guardians, and to report the facts of the case, to the Local Government Board. [Page 70]

6 September 1877. Ordered that the Clerk write to M$^r$ **Woods** of Holbeach to request him to enter into an agreement with the Guardians, to contribute towards his Son John's maintenance. [Page 70]

17 September 1877. Emily **Miller** was granted a leave of absence for a fortnight to visit M$^{rs}$ **Slater** of Tydd S. Mary. [Page 73]

4 October 1877. A letter from the Local Government Board re **Fenn** was read, and according to the direction therein, the Chairman cautioned the Master on the subject of refusing Paupers admission to the house in case of urgency after the house is closed. [Page 76]

4 October 1877. The Clerk was directed to write to C **Hardy** the contractor for coffins, and complain of the one made for William **Coleman**. [Page 76]

4 October 1877. The Clerk was directed to write to the Lincoln Union that the Guardians refused to admit Mary **Drakes** into the house without an order of Justices. [Page 76]

18 October 1877. A letter was read from the Rev$^d$ C. B. **Lowe**, Rector of Tydd, respecting the case of a woman named **Godfrey** and the Clerk was directed to acknowledge the receipt of his letter, and to assure him that the case would receive attention. [Page 80]

15 November 1877. An application was received from the Nottingham Guardians asking for an order to admit Susan **Francis** into the Workhouse and the Clerk ordered to refuse. [Page 83]

15 November 1877. A complaint was received from M$^{rs}$ **Nunn** an Inmate that the Medical Officer did not properly attend to her Grand-children the Master stated that M$^{rs}$ Nunn & her Grandchildren received every proper attention, and from the report of the Relieving Officer, the Master was directed in future to keep the children in the House when M$^{rs}$ Nunn discharged herself in order that they may be kept at school. [Page 83]

15 November 1877. Ordered that [*blank*] **Aspland** be called upon to pay towards the relief of his Father. [Page 83]

15 November 1877. Peter **Dolton** attended and complained that he was quite unable to pay towards the maintenance of his Father. Ordered that he pay 2/- a week. [Page 83]

13 December 1877. Ordered that the Clerk write M$^r$ R. R. **Harper** to give a report as to the state of Health of M$^{rs}$ **Nunns** Grandchildren who are supposed to be suffering from skin disease. [Page 87]

13 December 1877. Ordered that proceedings be taken against Job **Mawford** for non-maintenance and desertion of his wife. [Page 87]

13 December 1877. Ordered that George **Goddard** be called upon to pay 4$^s$/- a week towards the support of his wife now in the Lunatic Asylum. [Page 87]

13 December 1877. Leave of absence given to the **Tollidays** to visit. [Page 87]

27 December 1877. John **Holmes** – Common Charges – Removal of W. **Freeman** from Guy's
Hospital to Tydd St M.                         £1 18.3
Lunatic – E **Goddard**                        £2.19.9   [Page 89]

10 January 1878. An Order was made from the Hackney Union to remove M^rs E. **Harpham** and her five children and M^r **Marshall** was ordered to go to London & enquire into the matter & if necessary the Clerk was to give Notice of Appeal. [Page 92]

10 January 1878. Ordered that the Clerk make enquiries as to Hannah **Mawford**. [Page 92]

24 January 1878. R. O. **Mossop** – Common Chgs – Journey
          Jenny Louise **Mawford**       £1.10
Common Charges - Maintenance of W. **Freeman** in Guy's Hospital £9.12.0 [Page 93]

24 January 1878. M^r **Marshall** reported that he had made enquiries in relation to Emma **Harpham** & he recommended the Guardians to accept her. It was decided to contribute 5/- a week towards the support of Mrs Harpham and her family and to allow them to remain in their present Home in London, if the Hackney Guardians would pay her & charge the a/c to this Union. [Page 94]

24 January 1878. The Clerk reported that he had undertaken a Journey to Spalding and Terrington re **Mawford** and that he had found she was entitled to about 5a of Land and 1/3 of £1110 upon the death of her Mother & Mawford had signed an agreement to allow her 5/- a week so long as she remained chargeable and that he had offered if released from such payment to settle his wifes property upon her. The Guardians thought that the Family ought to accept this offer and maintain her but if they refuse to do so, Payment by Mawford was to be enforced. [Page 94]

7 February 1878. An application was heard from Elizabeth **Baxter** to obtain a Summons against John **Cayley** he being Father of her Bastard Child. [Page 96]

21 February 1878. The Clerk was ordered to write to James **Gibbs** of Tydd Gote and require him to pay towards the maintenance of his mother. [Page 97]

21 February 1878. The subject of the maintenance of Hannah **Mawford** was again considered and the Clerk directed to take steps to obtain a Settlement of Money due to her from her Husband. [Page 98]

7 March 1878. Ordered that the Clerk write to the Grimsby Union requesting their R. O. to allow William **Neal** 89 with 6/- weekly. [Page 100]

21 March 1878. Ordered that the Clerk write to Spalding Union requesting the R. O. of the Moulton District to continue the payment of 3/6 a week to Hannah **Pinder**. [Page 103]

21 March 1878l. At the request of the Boston Guardians an order was made for payment of Elizabeth **Leak** of 4/- a week until further notice. [Page 103]

4 April 1878. Ordered that the Clerk write to Spalding Union requesting the R. O. to allow Harriet **Buffham** aged 59 2/6 a week. [Page 105]

4 April 1878. On the application of Elizabeth **Baxter** it was ordered that a Summons be taken against [**Cayley** *in pencil*] the affiliation of her Bastard Child. [Page 105]

2 May 1878. Ordered that the Clerk apply to M^r Walter **Slator** for £4.18.3 expenses of removing Fanny Slator to the Asylum and that he pay the sum of 6/- a week towards her maintenance. [Page 113]

2 May 1878. Ordered that the Clerk write to M^r **Haines** enquiring why **Wilkinson**s name does not appear on his List. [Page 113]

16 May 1878. Common Charges – C. **Marshall** – exps fetching **Pilgram** from Coy Asylum £1.4.2 [Page 115]

16 May 1878. Ordered that a warrant be issued for Mary **Childs** if she does not remove her Bastard Child within a Week. [Page 115]

16 May 1878. Ordered that the Clerk inquire into the case of Jane **Whitehead** for the purpose of obtaining a removal order. [Page 115]

30 May 1878. Lunacy – J. **Holmes** – conveying J. **Wilson** to Asylum £3.11.6 [Page 117]

30 May 1878. W^m **Cayley** who deserted his children on the 3^rd August 1877 whereby they became chargeable to the Union now applies for leave to remove them, states he is not in a position to pay for <u>their</u> maintenance. The Board consented to allow him to take them out. [Page 117]

11 July 1878. Common Charges – J. **Holmes**    **Goddard**    £1.5.9
                                **Hammond**   £1.5.9   £2.11.6 [Page 124]

11 July 1878. The Clerk was directed to write to the Caistor Union to request the Guardians to pay Ann **Mills** 70 3/0 a week after 2^nd week of this quarter. [Page 125]

25 July 1878. Lunacy – C. **Marshall** – conveying Walter **Wells** to Lunatic Asylum £3.12.10 [Page 126]

25 July 1878. Ordered that the following Non Settled poor accounts be sent out. [Page 127]

| Lutton | **Holland** Harriet | 2/- per week | £1.6.0 |
| Peterboro' | **Muckling** Lavina | 3/6 per week | £2.5.6 |
| Wisbech | **Boor** Ann | 3/6 per week | 2.5.6 |
| Wisbech | **Dean** Mary | 4/- per week | 2.12.0  £4.17.6 |

8 August 1878. A report was read from M^r **Holmes** complaining that **Kime** had not supplied a proper coffin for Edward **Sharpe**, who was found drowned at Sutton St Marys, ordered that the Clerk write to Kime, and ask for an explanation. [Page 128]

8 August 1878. An order was made for the application of Jane **Whitehead**'s Bastard Child. [Page 129]

8 August 1878. Leave was given to the **Tolliday**s to visit their Uncle at Gedney Drove End for a month. [Page 129]

22 August 1878. An order for removal of Hannah **Bates** or **Betts** aged 14 years, from S^t George's Union Westminster was read, and the Clerk directed to obtain Copy of deposition, and inquire [*blank*] and if he finds any grounds give notice of appeal. [Page 131]

22 August 1878. The Master reported that Robert **Childs** aged 6 mo^s, had been again deserted by his mother. Ordered that proceedings be taken against Mary Ann Childs. [Page 131]

22 August 1878. Ordered that the Clerk write to Luton Union for 20/- for Clothes for Emma **Holland** on her going out as Domestic Servant to Mark **Cox**, Sutton Bridge Surveyor, at £3 per annum. [Page 131]

16 September 1878. Ellen **Tolliday** applied for the discharge of John Tolliday (her Nephew) which was granted. [Page 136]

3 October 1878. Ordered that the Collector collect from W^m **Sissey** 26/10 expenses of burying Benjamin Sissey. [Page 143]

3 October 1878. Ordered that the Clerk write to the Mother of Hannah **Betts**, that proceedings will be taken if she is not removed. [Page 143]

17 October 1878. Lunacy – J. **Holmes** -

| | re **Smith** | £3.5.9 | |
| | re **Patrick** | £2.6.3 | £5.12.0  [Page 144] |

17 October 1878. An application from M^rs **Gott** to let John & Charles **Sporton** have a fortnights leave was granted. [Page 145]

17 October 1878. The Clerk to write to Josiah **Wilson** of Gedney Cross Mill requiring him to come up next Board Day, relative to the Maintenance of his family, in the County Lunatic Asylum. [Page 145]

31 October 1878. Ordered that the Clerk apply to Richard **Kingerley** of Whaplode Farmer to pay 7/6 a week towards the Maintenance of his Grandchildren, children of Annie Kingerley Albert S^t Holbeach. [Page 146]

31 October 1878. Ordered that the Clerk apply to Tho^s **Clark** of Lutton to pay towards the Maintenance of Ann **Bradley**'s children. [Page 146]

31 October 1878. Josiah **Wilson** attended the Board and explained that he was totally unable to maintain his wife now in the County Lunatic Asylum. The property spoken of by M^r **Bettinson** does not belong to him. [Page 147]

14 November 1878. Report from M^r R. R. **Harper** was read as to **Cumberworth**, the Guardians direct that in cases similar to Cumberworths the M. O. must use his own discretion if the R. O. is from home, and they may rely on the Guardian's liberality. [Page 148]

14 November 1878. Ed **Mumby** having paid for the interment of his father, leave was given to him to take deceased's clothes. [Page 148]

14 November 1878. Tho^s **Clarke** attended the board as requested. Ordered to pay Ann **Bradley** & children 2/- per week or find a cottage for them. [Page 148]

14 November 1878. Rich^d **Kingerley** of Whaplode Farmer agrees to pay 7/6 per week, to his Grandchildren the children of Annie Kingerley. [Page 149]

14 November 1878. Ordered that the Clerk write to the Louth Board of Guardians asking them to receive Ann **Blanchard** aged 70 of Sutton Bridge (late of Batty's Passage Maiden Row Louth) a lunatic now in the County Asylum, without an order of justices. [Page 149]

14 November 1878. Ordered that the Clerk write to W^m **Dixon**'s two sons living at Peterboro to contribute to their father's maintenance. [Page 149]

14 November 1878. Ordered that Sarah **Taylor** a lunatic (in the Workhouse) be removed to the Asylum. [Page 149]

28 November 1878.   C. Chgs – J. **Holmes** -   re **Smith**         £1.6.9
                    Lunacy J. Holmes         re **Blanchard**   £3.19.0         £5.5.9  [Page 150]

28 November 1878. An order was made for the affiliation of Emma **Salter**'s bastard child. [Page 151]

26 December 1878. J. **Holmes** – Lunacy (re **Gee**) £3.7.9 [Page 154]

26 December 1878. Leave of absence was given to William **Cooper** an inmate for 7 days. [Page 155]

26 December 1878. Resolved that the amount paid for the maintenance of C. H. **Gee** be declared to be on Loan and that the Odd Fellows Society at Long Sutton be called upon to pay the amount due to Gee to the Collector of the Guardians as per Sec 23 of the Poor Law amendment Act of 1876. [Page 155]

9 January 1879. Ordered that M^r **Hart** apply for a warrant for Annie **Bingham** for deserting her children. [Page 157]

9 January 1879. Ordered that M^rs **Lane** have her husband's clothing. [Page 157]

23 January 1879. A letter was read from the Secr of the Odd Fellow's Society at Long Sutton relating to **Gee** and enclosing a copy of the resolution of the Society declining to acknowledge the claim made by the Guardians.
Resolved that a case be laid before M^r Sanderson **Tennant** for his opinion whether the Society could legally avoid the Act of Parliament by the Rule lately passed by them.
Ordered that the Clerk write to M^r **Dring** to bake the bread rather higher [Page 159]

6 February 1879. Louisa **Betts.** Ordered that the Clerk write to the Local Gov^t Board asking the sanction of their Lordships to pay 15^s/- to the Grantham Union for 21 days maintenance while under order of removal in December 1877. [Page 161]

6 February 1879. Charles & Matthew **Bilsby** and their families. Ordered that the Clerk inform the Guardians of the Rye Union in reply to their application that they decline to take these paupers without an order. [Page 161]

6 February 1879. **Bradley.** Ordered that the Clerk apply to Mr T **Clarke** calling upon him to contribute 1^s/6^d per week towards the Maintenance of his grandchild [*blank*] Bradley. [Page 161]

6 February 1879. Charlotte **Draper.** Ordered that the Clerk write to Miss **Ward** in reply informing her the Guardians would not advise in the matter. [Page 161]

6 February 1879. Robert **Eate.** Ordered that proceedings be taken to compel him to cause his child to be vaccinated. [Page 161]

20 February 1879. Lucy **Johnson.** Elizabeth Johnson attended and asked the Board to allow her to take her sister out of the house. Granted. [Page 163]

20 February 1879. **Bradley's** children. Mrs **Clarke** attended and informed the Board that her husband refused to contribute 1/6 per week towards the Maintenance of his grandchildren. Ordered that he be summoned to show cause why he should not contribute. [Page 163]

20 February 1879. **Harpham's** Children. Relieving Officer **Marshall** reported that he had made inquiries into this case and considered that M^rs Rose **Hicks** was a proper person to take charge of these children. And the Board consented to allow her 1/6 per week with each of them, one child to be left at Whaplode with M^r Harpham the grandfather. [Page 163]

20 February 1879. Charles Henry **Gee.** The opinion of M^r **Tennant** was read, he considered the Guardians had no practical remedy in this matter. [Page 163]

6 March 1879. L. **Simpson** – Lunacy re **Taylor**         £3.0.1
            Richd P **Mossop** – Common Chgs re **Bradley** £1.7.6  [Page 165]

6 March 1879. **Bradley's** Children. The clerk informed the Board the Magistrates refused to make an order in this case. [Page 165]

6 March 1879. Geo **Cooper.** John **Brewin** asked leave to take out this boy for a month on trial – granted. [Page 165]

6 March 1879. Emma **Watford.** Ordered that the Master apply to the Magistrates for a Warrant for the apprehension of Will^m Watford on the charge of deserting his wife Emma Watford whereby she became chargeable to this Union. [Page 165]

6 March 1879. Thomas **Carr.** Ordered that the R. O. inquire into the means of Thomas Carr of Holbeach Bank now chargeable. [Page 165]

6 March 1879. Hertford Union. Ordered that the Clerk write and ask the Guardians of the Hertford Union to pay Ann **Westmorland** aged 73 3/- per week from the 12<sup>th</sup> week of this Quarter on the A/<sup>c</sup> of this Union. [Page 165]

6 March 1879. Wisbech Union re Mary **Dean**. Ordered that the Clerk write and ask the Guardians of the Wisbech Union to take this woman she being a non resident pauper belonging to them having fallen ill and being unable to take care of herself. [Page 165]

20 March 1879. Thomas **Carr**. Miss Carr attended and informed the Board that her father had spent all his money as far as she knew and that her brothers were not in a position to maintain him. [Page 170]

20 March 1879. re **Peek** a Lunatic. M<sup>r</sup> Thomas Peek attended the Board and explained that his Brother had some money when he was taken to the Asylum and that after paying for his removal there was quite £106.12.0 left. Ordered that this sum be paid to the Treasurer and applied to the lunatic's maintenance. [Page 170]

20 March 1879. Lydia **Grange**. Ordered that the Clerk inquire whether any money is due to this woman, under Henry **Baker**'s Will. [Page 170]

20 March 1879. re John **Bloy**. Ordered on the application of the Caistor Union, that this Union do admit that this lunatic is chargeable, and that the Clerk write to Bracebridge informing them to charge him to this Union instead of the Caistor Union. [Page 170]

20 March 1879. re Robert **Parkins**. Ordered that the Clerk apply for the deposition in this case and notice of appeal be given in due course to the S<sup>t</sup> Pancras Union. [Page 170]

20 March 1879. Elizabeth **Mason** a lunatic. Ordered that M<sup>r</sup> K. **Folley** be called upon to contribute towards the maintenance of this person. [Page 170]

20 March 1879. Wisbech Union re Mary **Dean**. The Clerk informed the Board that this pauper had been removed. [Page 170]

3 April 1879. **Peek** – amt paid in towards his maintenance in Asylum    106.2.0 [Page 171]

3 April 1879. W<sup>m</sup> **Beck** an inmate applied for assistance to go and seek work. 4lbs bread granted. [Page 172]

3 April 1879. **Limbert**. Ordered that the Clerk ask the sanction of the Local Govt Board to the payment to M<sup>r</sup> R. R. **Harper** of the sum of £2 for his services in extracting a stone from the pipe of the penis of a boy named Isaac Limbert aged 8 years. [Page 172]

17 April 1879. **Smith**. Ordered that M<sup>r</sup> **Hart** apply to the Magistrates for a Warrant for Smith for deserting her child Patsey Smith whereby she became chargeable. [Page 178]

1 May 1879. **Bycroft** attended the Board and asked to have a boy on trial for a month. Granted take **Hayes**. [Page 180]

1 May 1879. Emily **Eke**, an inmate (in the infirmary) is subject to epilepsy with manical paroxysom and requires attention, on the recommendation of the Doctor, the Master was ordered to provide assistance to look after her. [Page 180]

1 May 1879. **Roof**. Ordered that Roof be allowed to go out of the house without taking his wife. [Page 181]

15 May 1879. C **Marshall** - Comm Chgs – removing **Wells** & **Taylor** from Asylum £1.11.0 [Page 182]

15 May 1879. Wisbech Union. A letter was read from the Wisbech Union asking us to receive Francis **Revell** a Blacksmith aged 78 years without an order of Justices, he about 20 years ago rented a Public House known as the Red Last and 4 acres of Land adjoining at Whaplode.
The Guardians being satisfied that he belonged to this Union agreed to accept him without an order. [Page 182]

15 May 1879. Caistor Union. A letter from the Caistor Union was read asking us to advance William **Neal** 1/- per week on account of sickness.
The Guardians refused to pay this proposed increase, he at the present is receiving top relief and has children able to assist him. [Page 182]

15 May 1879. Anthony **Johnson**. W<sup>m</sup> **Tickler** of Moulton & his apprentice Anthony **Jackson** attended the Board and asked to have the Indentures cancelled. Ordered that the Indentures be cancelled on the payment of 5/- to the boy by the Master. [Page 182]

12 June 1879. re **Parkins**. The Clerk informed the Board that the Guardians of the St Pancras Union had abandoned this appeal. [Page 186]

12 June 1879. re William **Clarke**. The Clerk informed the Board that the Magistrates had given judgement in their favour. [Page 186]

12 June 1879. re Geo **Cooper**. M^r **Brewin** and George Cooper attended the Board, the boy expressed his willingness to live with M^r Brewin. Resolved that he have an outfit of £2. [Page 186]

12 June 1879. re F^k **Hayes**. Mr **Bycroft** & Fred^k Hayes attended the Board and agreed to take F^k Hayes as servant for one year. Resolved he have an outfit of £2. [Page 186]

12 June 1879. re **Watte**. Ordered that proceedings be taken against Abraham Watte for the arrears of payment due under his agreement. [Page 187]

12 June 1879. W^m **Thompson**. The Master was directed to take proceedings against William Thompson for neglecting to maintain Malenda Thompson his wife. [Page 187]

26 June 1879. re **Watte**. The Collector reported that Watte had paid him £1.12.0 on a/c and the Guardians consented to give him further time. [Page 189]

26 June 1879. re **Morfitt**. Ordered that the Master apply to the Magistrate for a Warrant for the apprehension of Job **Mawford** for deserting his Wife and Child whereby they became chargeable to this Union. [Page 189]

26 June 1879. Sarah Ann Sell aged 43 & 3 children applied for Relief, she having only just come to live in this Union. Ordered that the R. O. inquire into this case, and find to what Union she does belong she stating that she was born at Langtoft in the Bourn Union, & married there to George **Sells** of that place.
Ordered that the Clerk write and ask the Bourn Union to receive her without an order of Juctices. [Page 189]

26 June 1879. re Fanny **Slator** a Lunatic in the County Asylum. A letter from Walter Slator her husband was read informing the Board that he would no longer contribute towards the maintenance of his wife, he having applied to the Visitors for her discharge but they would not comply with his request.
Ordered that the Clerk inform him that in the crowded state of the Asylum that he might rest assured that the Authorities will grant her discharge as soon as it is wise to do so, and that in the meantime he must contribute towards her maintenance.
Ordered also that the Clerk write to the Medical Superintendent as to the state of her health. [Page 190]

26 June 1879. **Childs**. Ordered that the R. O. inquire where the mother of Martha Childs is. [Page 190]

10 July 1879. Matilda **Walker**. The master reported this woman for wilfully neglecting the regulations by accusing Frances **Joyce** one of the other inmates of disreputable conduct and using bad language in the aged women's day room. Francis Joyce attended & complained. Ordered that she be taken before the Magistrates. [Page 192]

10 July 1879. re M^rs **Gresham**. A letter from M^r John **Flooks** was read complaining that M^rs **Ironmonger** compels her mother M^rs Gresham (a pauper) to keep her bed and take her clothes away from her. Ordered that R. O. **Marshall** inquire and report. [Page 192]

10 July 1879. re M^rs **Drury**. A letter from the Rev^d Rob^t K. **Arbuthnot** was read asking the Board to give her a little support. Ordered that wine be given when ordered by the Medical Officer. [Page 192]

24 July 1879. M r **Millns** the Collector reported that Rob^t **Ringham** was not able to pay 2/- per week towards the maintenance of his son John F. Ringham an inmate in the Bracebridge Asylum. Ordered that he be not as heretofore. [Page 194]

24 July 1879. re **Parkins**. The Clerk informed the Board that he had recd notice to produce the Board's Minute Book at the taxing of the Costs. Ordered that the Clerk attend with it if it is necessary to produce it. [Page 194]

24 July 1879. re Fanny **Slator**. M^r W. Slator attended and requested the Guardians to consent to his wife being removed from the Asylum to live with him. The Guardians after considering the case came to the conclusion that she was under better care & treatment than he could afford her, so did not grant his request, but ordered that he pay 5^s/- per week instead of 6^s/- towards her maintenance. [Page 194]

24 July 1879. re Rob^t **Bingham**. Ordered that the Clerk write & ask the sanction of the Local Gov^t Board to the payment of £2 to D^r **Crowden** for amputating the finger of Rob^t Bingham, he not

having obtained a certificate from some other Medical Man that such amputation was necessary before performing the operation, but has since obtained one from D[r] **Stiles** of Spalding. [Page 194]

24 July 1879. re M[rs] **Gresham**. R:O: Marshall informed the Board that he had inquired into this case and found that M[rs] Gresham was properly taken care of by her daughter M[rs] **Ironmonger** & that Mr **Flookes** was satisfied. [Page 194]

24 July 1879. re **Gibbs**. The Board allowed this man time to pay the amount now due to the Guardians. [Page 194]

7 August 1879. Re **Ringham**. Ordered that the Clerk request Rob[t] Ringham to attend the next Meeting of the Board & that R.O. Marshall inquire into the case. [Page 196]

7 August 1879. re **Wright**. Ordered that Jerimiah Wright attend the next Meeting of the Guardians to show cause why he should not contribute to the maintenance of his father. [Page 196]

7 August 1879. Spalding Union. A letter from the Spalding Union was read asking us to pay on their a/c Bridget **Lee** 74 years of age 3[s]/6[d] per week after 4th Week this Quarter. Ordered that R.O. **Marshall** pay it until further notice. [Page 197]

7 August 1879. Sarah Ann Sells & Children. Ordered that no more Out Relief be given to these paupers, & that the house be offered, and if she becomes chargeable the Clerk obtain an Order for Removal. [Page 197]

7 August 1879. re **Richards**. M[rs] Richards attended and informed the Board that her husband was obliged to give up business and he can no longer pay towards the maintenance of his daughter in the Asylum. Ordered that he no longer be called upon to pay and the back money be forgiven. [Page 197]

7 August 1879. re Fanny **Slator**. A letter from the Clerk of the County Asylum was read informing this Board that Fanny Slator had on the 29th Ult been discharged, and that her husband (Walter Slator) had signed an undertaking as required by the Act, to the satisfaction of the Committee, that his wife (Fanny Slator) shall no longer be chargeable & shall be properly taken care of and shall be prevented from doing an injury to herself or others. [Page 197]

7 August 1879. Leeds Union. Letters from the Clerk of the Leeds Union were read asking the Guardians of this Union to accept Elizabeth **Dickerson**, a lunatic, without an order of justices. Ordered that the Clerk inform the Leeds Union that the Guardians refuse to accept her without an Order of Justices as they do not consider she belongs to this Union. [Page 197]

21 August 1879. re **Ringham**. Robert Ringham attended and explained to the Board that he was quite unable to contribute towards the Maintenance of his son in the County Asylum, he also stated that he had never received any application from the Collector for any money. The Guardians were satisfied that he could not pay and ordered the Clerk to inform the Local Gov[t] Board of the statement made by Ringham "that he had received no application from the Collector for the payment of the money he agreed to pay". The Collector was not present & the clerk was directed to report to the L.G.B. that the collector had not attended the last 2 meetings. [Page 199]

21 August 1879. re **Wright**. Jeremiah Wright, Brickmaker and Machinist attended and agreed to pay 1[s]/- per week towards his Father's maintenance. [Page 199]

21 August 1879. re **Needham**. Ordered that M[r] **Hart** apply to the Magistrates for a Warrant for William Edward Needham for deserting his wife & child whereby they became chargeable to this Union. [Page 200]

21 August 1879. Horncastle Union. Ordered the Clerk ask the Guardians of the Horncastle Union to pay Jarvis **Stanch** 77 years 3[s]/6[d] per week on a/c of this Union until further notice. [Page 200]

4 September 1879. Boston Union. Ordered that the Clerk ask the Guardians of the Boston Union to pay W[m] **Harrison** 3/6 weekly after the 10th Week of this Quarter on the a/c of this Union until further notice. [Page 203]

4 September 1879. re **Childs**. Ordered that R.O. **Holmes** take proceedings against John Childs for having wilfully neglected to provide proper food and clothing for his wife and two children, whereby they had to be removed to the workhouse. [*In the margin in pencil*] Sent to prison 1 months hard labour. [Page 203]

4 September 1879. re **Gibbs**. Ordered that the Clerk inform the Collector Ann Gibbs died 30th Aug[t] last. [Page 203]

18 September 1879. – C. **Ingamells** – Com Chgs – **Holmes** 2 childs [Page 205]

18 September 1879. re M[rs] **Bennett**. Ordered that the Clerk inquire into the Paternity of M[rs] Bennett's bastard child. [Page 206]

16 October 1879. re Sarah **Bennett**. Ordered that an information be laid against Thomas Woolstone Seaton **Loweth** of Stamford a Land Surveyor whom she alleges to be the father of her child. [Page 209]

16 October 1879. re **Mason**. R. K. **Folley** attended and the Board consented to reduce his contribution to 5[s]/- a week commencing from the time she became chargeable. [Page 212]

16 October 1879. re **Whitby**. Ordered that Edward Whitby of Lime Walk Lutton meet the Board next Board Day to show cause why he should not contribute towards the maintenance of his wife an inmate in the County Asylum, Bracebridge. [Page 212]

[undated] . Isaac **Peek**, Cost of maintenance at the County Asylum £12.10.5
Com Chgs D[r] to Isaac Peek Cr 11s/ refunded [Page 213]

30 October 1879. re **Bennett**. The Clerk reported Thomas W. S. **Loweth** was ordered to pay 2[s]/- a week towards the maintenance of Sarah Bennett's child. [Page 217]

30 October 1879. re **Whitby**. Ed. Whitby attended and agreed to pay 2[s]/- a week towards the maintenance of his wife. [Page 217]

30 October 1879. re **Groom**. Ordered that M[r] **Hart** obtain one pair of Elastic Stockings for Mary Groom. [Page 217]

30 October 1879. Spalding Union. On the application of the Spalding Union the Clerk was ordered to forward an order for the admission of Hannah **Watson** into this Workhouse. [Page 217]

13 November 1879. Coffin Contractor. Ordered that the Clerk write to M[r] **Kime** with respect to the coffin for Richard **Collins** of Whaplode, M[rs] **Collins** having complained that the coffin was not large enough, and she had been obliged to get another Carpenter M[r] **Dickinson** to enlarge it who charged her 3/-. [Page 220]

13 November 1879. re Joseph **Gull**. Ordered that his relief be paid through the Sleaford Union. [Page 220]

27 November 1879. Coffin Contractors. M[r] **Kime** attended and informed the Board that the Coffin made for **Collins** dec[d] was large enough, but as M[rs] Collins had to obtain the assistance of another Carpenter he agreed to pay the 3/- charged to her. [Page 223]

27 November 1879. **Carr**. Ordered that Robert **Young** have Thomas Carrs' dec[d] crutches. [Page 223]

11 December 1879. Sells & child. The Clerk informed the Board that the Guardians of the Bourn Union had forwarded an order for the admission of the above pauper into their Union Workhouse. [Page 226]

11 December 1879. Hannah **Pinder**. Ordered that the Clerk ask the Guardians of the Spalding Union to pay this woman aged 75 years 3/6 per week after the 11th week of the Quarter, on a/c of this Union. [Page 227]

24 December 1879. J. **Holmes** – Lunacy – conveying E. **Whitby** from Asylum £1.7.3 [Page 229]

24 December 1879. Sheffield Union. A letter was read asking the Guardians to sanction an advance of 1[s]/- per week to Joseph **Jackson** through increased infirmities. Granted. [Page 230]

24 December 1879. Spalding Union re Thomas **Luff**. A letter from the Spalding Union was read asking the Guardians to receive this man without an order. Ordered that the clerk reply the Guardians are not satisfied that he belongs to them so cannot accept him.
Re Harriett **Pinder**. A letter was also read from the Spalding Union stating that the house at Moulton where this woman was going to reside was overcrowded, therefore they did not feel justified in permitting their Officer to pay the relief in question. [Page 230]

8 January 1880. re **Alford**. Ordered that R O **Holmes** pay M[r] **Naylor** the overseer who paid for the burial of Henry Alford who was found at Sutton Bridge drowned, the full allowance which he pays at ordinary funerals. [Page 235]

8 January 1880. re **Foreman**. Ordered that the Clerk write and ask the Spalding Union to pay Mary Foreman 67 3[s]/6[d] per week after 4th week this Quarter on A/C of this Union. [Page 235]

8 January 1880. re **Dean** Blind. D[r] **Vise** informed the Board that Maria Dean would be received into the University College for the benefit of her eyes. Ordered that she be removed. [Page 235]

22 January 1880. C. **Marshall** – Com Charges - Exp[s] incurred removing Maria **Dean** to hospital £1.9.3
J. **Holmes** – Lunacy – Exp[s] conveying **Mallet** to the Asylum £3.14.9 [Page 238]

22 January 1880. Birmingham Union. A letter from Birmingham Union was read asking the Guardians to receive Thomas **Watson** 60 years without an order. Ordered that R. O. **Marshall** inquire into the case. [Page 239]

5 February 1880. J. **Holmes** – Com Charges – Exp$^s$ removing Hannah **Atkinson** (blind) from Guy's Hospital to Long Sutton [Page 242]

5 February 1880. re **Rodwell**. On the recommendation of the Medical Officer it was resolved to remove Mary Rodwell to Guy's Hospital. [Page 243]

5 February 1880. re Nathan **Mackinder**. It was reported to the Board that the sum of £31.10.0 was due to Nathan Mackinder (now chargeable) from George Mackinder Shoemaker Holbeach Bank. Ordered that the Clerk call upon him to attend the next Meeting, and explain the matter. [Page 243]

5 February 1880. re George **Hinton**. Ordered that the Clerk write to M$^r$ R. R. **Harper** to report on this case at the next meeting. [Page 243]

5 February 1880. re Thomas **Watson**. R O. **Marshall** reported he had inquired into this case and that he found this man was not known at Gedney Hill or in the neighbourhood. Ordered that the Clerk reply the Guardians cannot accept him without an Order of Justice. [Page 243]

19 February 1880. re **Chamberlain**. Ordered that the Clerk call upon William Chamberlain to contribute 2$^s$/6$^d$ per week towards the maintenance of his Father and Mother now chargeable. [Page 247]

19 February 1880. M$^{rs}$ **Enderby** applied to see **King** an inmate, she not being related the application was refused. [Page 247]

19 February 1880. J. **Holmes** – Com. Charges. Exps. incurred removing Fanny **Hazel** from hospital £1.12.11 [Page 247]

19 February 1880. C. **Marshall** – Expenses incurred removing M. **Rodwell** from Whaplode to Guys Hospital £1.18.11 [Page 247]

19 February 1880. Hannah **Watson** an inmate applied for a pair of boots for her boy, and to leave her girl in the house. Application refused. [Page 248]

19 February 1880. Eliza **Needham** asked if the Board could find her husband. She was informed that a warrant had been issued, but the Police had not found him. [Page 248]

19 February 1880. re Owen **Clusky**. The Clerk informed the Board that an inquest was held at the Workhouse on the 14$^{th}$ February last by M$^r$ Selby, on the body of Owen Clusky who was brought to the Union on the previous Thursday in a dying state. The Verdict was that dec$^d$ died from Natural Cause, inflammation of the lungs. [Page 248]

19 February 1880. re Nathan **Mackinder**. Geo Mackinder attended and signed an Agreement to pay 2/6 per week towards the maintenance of Nathan Mackinder now chargeable. [Page 248]

4 March 1880. C. **Marshall** – Com Charges – convey. J. **Rodwell** from Hospital £1.14.3
Also – Lunacy – conveying **Oldridge** to the Asylum £3.0.4 [Page 250]

4 March 1880. Spalding Union re **Gull**. A letter from the Spalding Union was read asking to pay this man's relief as heretofore. Granted. [Page 251]

4 March 1880. Guardians v **Clarke**. Ordered that an execution be issued for the recovery of the amt now owing Clarke having failed to comply with the Order of the judge. [Page 251]

4 March 1880. Ordered that the Clerk call upon George **Goodwin** Wheelwright Long Sutton to contribute 3$^s$/- per week towards the maintenance of his father John **Fountain** Blacksmith Long Sutton to contribute 3$^s$/- per week towards the maintenance of his mother and David **Osbourn**, Barber Long Sutton to contribute 3$^s$/- per week towards the maintenance of his mother. [Page 252]

4 March 1880. re **Atkins** Bastard Child. Ordered that the Clerk inquire whether there is sufficient evidence to obtain an order against the alleged father. [Page 252]

18 March 1880. re Fanny **Slator**. A letter from Walter Slator was read asking the Guardians to forgive the arrears amounting to £4.4.0 due from him for the maintenance of his wife while an inmate of the County Asylum. Resolved that further time be granted. [Page 257]

18 March 1880. re **Atkin's** Bastard Child. Ordered that no summons in this case be applied for. [Page 257]

18 March 1880. re **Osborne**. A letter from D. Osborne was read stating that he was unable to contribute 3/- per week towards the maintenance of his mother. Resolved that he pay 1/6 per week and his brother Charles be called upon to pay 1/6 per week. [Page 257]

18 March 1880. re **Fountain**. R O **Holmes** reported that M<sup>rs</sup> Fountain had discontinued to receive relief. [Page 257]

18 March 1880. re **Goodwin**. Ordered that Goodwin be summoned to show cause why he should not contribute towards the maintenance of his father. [Page 258]

18 March 1880. re **Dolton**. Ordered that Peter Dolton be called upon to pay the amount of arrears now due. [Page 258]

18 March 1880. re **Cook**. Ordered that Joseph Cook Junr be called upon to contribute towards the maintenance of Joseph Cook Snr. [Page 258]

18 March 1880. re **Hardy**. Ordered that John Hardy be called upon to contribute 2/6 per week towards the maintenance of his mother Ann Hardy. [Page 258]

18 March 1880. Peterborough Union re **Money** & her 3 children. In September last this woman was allowed relief by the Peterboro Union to be paid by our Relieving Officer but she never applied until last Week when she attended the Board and was granted 4/6 per week from 13 Week this quarter subject to Peterboro Union repaying us the same. [Page 258]

1 April 1880. re **Goodwin**. Ordered that George Goodwin be summoned to show cause why he should not contribute towards the maintenance of his father. [Page 261]

1 April 1880. re **Cook**. Ordered that an order for the House be given to Cook. [Page 261]

1 April 1880. re **Wright**. Ordered that Jeremiah Wright be put into the County Court for the recovery of the amount of arrears now due from him. [Page 261]

1 April 1880. re **Watte**. Collector **Marshall** reported Watte had paid £1 on A/C. Resolved that further time be granted. [Page 261]

1 April 1880. W<sup>m</sup> **Dixon** an inmate applied for a pair of shoes. Refused. [Page 261]

1 April 1880. Edward **Bycraft** thatcher Whaplode asked leave of the Board to take Arthur **Watson** (an inmate) as servant, the boy attended and stated he should like to go. Ordered that he go for one month on trial. [Page 262]

1 April 1880. Peterboro Union re **Money** & children. A letter from the Peterborough Union was read sanctioning the amount of Relief granted by this Board on their Account to these paupers. [Page 262]

1 April 1880. re **Ford**. A letter from M<sup>r</sup> **Exby** was read informing the Board that Elizth Ford (late a recipient of Relief but now residing at Wisbech) was ready to go into service and obtained a situation but her Aunt with whom she resides has not the means to provide her with suitable clothing and asking the Board to grant her the usual outfit. Ordered that the Clerk inform M<sup>r</sup> Exby that she must make application through the Wisbech Union. [Page 262]

15 April 1880. C. **Marshall** – Com. Chgs. – Expenses incurred removing **Green** from Hospital £1.18.9 [Page 266]

15 April 1880. re **Gardiner**. Ordered that Elizabeth Gardiner go as Servant for one month on trial to M<sup>r</sup> N. **Wright**. [Page 267]

15 April 1880. re **Cooper**. Ordered that the Master apply for a warrant for the apprehension of *blank* Cooper for deserting his wife and child whereby they became chargeable to this Union. [Page 267]

15 April 1880. re **M<sup>c</sup>Gregor**. Ordered that the Clerk call upon John M and Charles M<sup>c</sup>Gregor to contribute 1/6 each per week towards the maintenance of their father John M<sup>c</sup>Gregor aged 74 years now chargeable. [Page 267]

15 April 1880. Mary **Freeman**. Ordered that the Clerk write and ask the Wisbech Union to accept this pauper without an Order, as soon as she can be safely removed. She came into this Workhouse a few weeks ago pregnant and was born at Wisbech in 1860. [Page 267]

29 April 1880. C. **Marshall** –     Com. Chgs. Re **Dean**          £1.16.9
                                                  Lunacy re **Gay**              £3.0 10     £4.17.7 [Page 270]

29 April 1880. re William **Cooper**. The Guardians are willing to release this man on his paying the cost of his Wife's maintenance viz:- 22<sup>s</sup>/6<sup>d</sup>. [Page 271]

29 April 1880. re **Hazel**. R O **Holmes** reported that this Girl (who he took to the Hospital some time ago) was now chargeable to the Greenwich Union. Resolved that she be fetched home. [Page 271]

29 April 1880. re **Helstrip**. Ordered that the Clerk write the Commanding Officer Malitia informing him that the Wife and children of Edward Helstrip are now chargeable to this Union and asking that the money due to Helstrip may be forwarded to us. [Page 271]

13 May 1880. re **Rodwell**. R O **Marshall** informed the Board that he rec$^d$ from Guys Hopsital, a notice requiring him to fetch Mary Rodwell home for a short space, which he had done. [Page 273]

13 May 1880. J. **Holmes**          expenses re **Hazel**          £1.13.7

C. **Marshall**          expenses re **Rodwell**          £1.17.9   [Page 274]

13 May 1880. re **Gainsley**. Ordered that the Clerk write Benjamin Bristow Gainsley to contribute 5$^s$/- per week towards the maintenance of his son Benjamin Gainsley and his 4 children. [Page 275]

13 May 1880. re **M$^c$Gregor**. A letter from Charles M$^c$Gregor was read stating that he was willing to contribute 1/6 per week towards his father's maintenance. Ordered that this be accepted & that R O **Holmes** make further inquiry as to the ability of his brother John M$^c$Gregor to contribute 1/6 per week also. [Page 275]

27 May 1880. re Arthur **Watson**. Edward **Bycroft** attended and stated that he was willing to take into his service for one year Arthur Watson aged 14 years and to pay him £2 as wages. Resolved that he be allowed £2 to procure the usual outfit. [Page 277]

27 May 1880. re George **Jessop**. The Master reported that George Jessop decd late an inmate of the Workhouse who died there was insured with the Prudential Company for £19.19.0 and that his wife resident in Yorkshire had made application for the Certificate of his death. Ordered that the Clerk apply for £9.11.9 being the cost of deceased maintenance. [Page 277]

27 May 1880. re **Ettridge** decd. The wife of Etteridge applied for the clothes of her late husband. Granted. [Page 277]

27 May 1880. re Elizabeth **Gardner**. M$^{rs}$ **Wright** agrees to take Elizabeth Gardner an inmate of the Workhouse as domestic Servant for 12 months, and to pay her 50/- wages. Ordered that the same amount be expended in providing her with the necessary outfit. [Page 277]

27 May 1880. re Emma **Parsons**. Ordered that M$^r$ **Hart** apply to the Magistrates for a warrant for the apprehension of John Tobias Parsons for neglecting to maintain his wife Emma Parsons whereby she became chargeable to this Union. [Page 277]

27 May 1880. re Alice **Brightman**. Ordered that the Clerk write the father of Alice Brightman requesting him to remove his daughter out of the house immediately. [Page 277]

27 May 1880. re Maria **Deans**. Ordered that the Clerk write the House Surgeon University College Hospital when Maria Deans can be re admitted. [Page 277]

| Name | Page | Name | Page |
|------|------|------|------|
| Adams | 22,23(3) | Boatwright | 35,36,40(2) |
| Aldred | 38 | Boor | 10,11,16,18,43 |
| Alford | 48 | Booth | 2 |
| Allwood | 22 | Boulding | 1,10 |
| Amory | 21 | Bowers | 11(2) |
| Anderson | 3,32,34 | Boyce | 21 |
| Andrews | 20(2) | Brace | 21,35 |
| Arbuthnot | 46 | Bradley | 21,43(2),44(4) |
| Arthburthnot | 31 | Braybrook | 38 |
| Arnold | 25,26 | Brett | 8 |
| Arnsby | 24 | Brewin | 38,44,46 |
| Aspland | 41 | Bridgeman | 23 |
| Atkins | 49(2) | Brightman | 26,51 |
| Atkinson | 7,49 | Brittain | 36 |
| Atwood | 23(2) | Brook | 4,6 |
| Aucock | 20,30,32 | Brown | 17,30,32,39 |
| Ayliff | 15,27 | Buffham | 12,42 |
|  |  | Bugg | 4 |
| Bailey | 2 | Bull | 14 |
| Baker | 45 | Bunn | 14 |
| Ball | 39 | Burgess | 2,4(2) |
| Balls | 3,39 | Burrell | 5,30 |
| Banks | 41 | Burton | 21 |
| Barker | 12,32,36 | Bush | 24,28(2) |
| Barnes | 3,10(2) | Butcher | 22,26,36,37 |
| Barrat | 29 | Bycraft | 50 |
| Barratt | 31 | Bycroft | 28,40(2),45,46,51 |
| Bates | 43 | Byron | 2 |
| Baxter | 2,6,12,14,34,42(2) |  |  |
| Beach | 8 | Caparn | 32,33(2) |
| Beard | 19 | Carbutt | 1,33 |
| Beck | 45 | Cardell | 22,31 |
| Beckett | 11 | Cardwell | 38 |
| Beckey | 15 | Carr | 44,45,48 |
| Bell | 8,12,21,23,26 | Carter | 12,38 |
| Bellairs | 7 | Cartwright | 4 |
| Bennet | 36(2) | Cave | 11,36 |
| Bennett | 3,6,9(2),12,14,15(2),16(2), | Cayley | 42(3) |
|  | 17,18,20,21(2),24,31,33(2),35(2), | Chamberlain | 15,16,17(2),21,49 |
|  | 36,38,39,48(3) | Chambers | 24,40 |
| Bett | 22,28(2) | Chapman | 32,36 |
| Bettinson | 43 | Chappe | 10 |
| Betts | 2,3(2),19,24,30,43(2),44 | Chartes | 17 |
| Biggadike | 1(3) | Chettle | 32(2),33 |
| Bills | 21 | Child | 39 |
| Bilsby | 44 | Childs | 16(2),42,43,46,47 |
| Bingham | 44,46 | Chiltern | 28 |
| Birch | 34(2) | Christmas | 30 |
| Blackster | 35 | Christopher | 21,22,29 |
| Blanchard | 43,44 | Clark | 39,43 |
| Blower | 1,15,18,33,35 | Clarke | 1,4,15(2),19,21,39,40,43,44(2), |
| Bloy | 41,45 |  | 46,49 |
| Blundy | 6 | Clay | 27 |
| Boardman | 38 | Clifton | 40 |

| Name | Page |
|---|---|
| Mabletoft | 2,7(2),8,12 |
| Mackharness | 17 |
| Mackinder | 49(2) |
| Mackman | 8(2),10 |
| Mair | 35 |
| Mallet | 48 |
| Mallows | 16 |
| Manton | 10(2),11,31 |
| Mapletoft | 14 |
| Marshall | 9,10,13,15(2),16,19,23,24, |
| | 29,31,36,38,42(4),44,45,46,47(3) |
| | 48,49(4),50(3),51(2) |
| Martin | 36 |
| Mason | 45,48 |
| Mawford | 41,42(4),46 |
| Maxwell | 14 |
| May | 2,15(2),32,34(2) |
| McGregor | 50,51 |
| Meatheringham | 8 |
| Meek | 11 |
| Mellor | 21,36,37 |
| Mellors | 35 |
| Miller | 41 |
| Millns | 4,36,38(2),46 |
| Mills | 42 |
| Money | 38,50(2) |
| Morfitt | 46 |
| Mossop | 42,44 |
| Mowbray | 33 |
| Muckling | 16,43 |
| Mumby | 5,6,38(2), 40(2),43 |
| Munson | 1 |
| Murfitt | 7 |
| | |
| Naylor | 5,11,20,48 |
| Neagle | 15 |
| Neal | 42,45 |
| Needham | 47,49 |
| Neville | 3 |
| Nicholls | 9,11,12,14 |
| Nidd | 3,7,8(2),24,25(2),26(2) |
| Nunn | 40,41(2) |
| | |
| Oldridge | 49 |
| Oliver | 40 |
| Osborne | 49 |
| Osbourn | 49 |
| Ouzman | 9 |
| | |
| Palmer | 3,4(2),5(3),9,10(2),11(2), |
| | 30,31(3) |
| Panks | 27(2) |
| Pape | 34,35(2) |
| Papworth | 5(2) |

| Name | Page |
|---|---|
| Parkins | 45(2),46 |
| Parkinson | 3 |
| Parks | 14 |
| Parr | 9,12(2),29 |
| Parrot | 2 |
| Parsons | 28(2),29,34,40,51 |
| Patman | 15(3) |
| Patrick | 43 |
| Peach | 28 |
| Pearman | 1,2 |
| Peck | 9,10 |
| Peek | 45(2),48 |
| Pepper | 38 |
| Perkins | 7(2),13 |
| Pesterfield | 30 |
| Pickett | 6,39 |
| Pidd | 22,23(2) |
| Pilgram | 42 |
| Pilgrim | 39 |
| Pinder | 42,48(2) |
| Pitts | 32 |
| Plowright | 29,31 |
| Pollin | 27 |
| Porter | 2,7(2),8,12,14(2),34,40 |
| Proctor | 4 |
| | |
| Rawlings | 12 |
| Rea | 14 |
| Read | 3 |
| Redhead | 10 |
| Reed | 3(2),37(2) |
| Remington | 29 |
| Revell | 45 |
| Richards | 18(3),20(2),39,47 |
| Riches | 38 |
| Rickett | 20,22 |
| Rigall | 6(2) |
| Riggal | 6 |
| Ringham | 28,46,47(2) |
| Rippin | 21 |
| Rising | 8,12 |
| Roberts | 15(2),16 |
| Robinson | 8,31,35 |
| Rodwell | 49(3),51(2) |
| Rodyers | 40 |
| Rogers | 26(2),40 |
| Rolfe | 4 |
| Roof | 10,45 |
| Roony | 10 |
| Roper | 7 |
| Roughton | 28 |
| Rowden | 34 |
| Rowe | 29,30(2) |
| Rowshan | 14 |

| | |
|---|---|
| Acknowledge(d) | e.g. "Casterton Magna having refused to acknowledge her". The parish of Casterton Magna did not accept that she could claim a settlement there. In most cases it would be requested that a removal order be issued for the pauper; the parish to which the pauper was removed would then be able to appeal against the order, the pauper would be examined as to her place of settlement and the settlement would be proved one way or the other. |
| Affiliation | Where bastardy was concerned, once the paternity of a bastard child had been proved, an affiliation order, or bastardy order, was made requiring the father to pay so much a week, and costs, for a stated number of years. |
| Attach | e.g. "he would attach 6<sup>s</sup>/- out of his wages towards their support". The amount of money involved would be taken from the wages by the employer and sent to the Union. |
| Belonging to | Is legally settled in. |
| Board of Guardians | See introduction. |
| Chargeable to | e.g. "chargeable to that parish" – the pauper needs poor relief from the parish where he resides which may or may not be his place of legal settlement. |
| Clothing | Paupers in the workhouse were supplied with several articles of clothing, often made in the workhouse. Their own clothes were kept and returned to them when they left the workhouse. |
| Clubs | Many people belonged to local sick clubs or Friendly Societies such as the Oddfellows. These clubs paid out so much per week during times of sickness to subscribers, and also paid a set sum after a subscriber died. |
| Common Fund | See Establishment. |
| Establishment | Also called "Common Fund" or "General Fund" – the general fund of the workhouse. |
| General Fund | See Establishment. |
| Guardians | See introduction. |
| House | "The House" i.e. the workhouse. |
| In case | e.g. "in case he should be considered able to support his mother", meaning "if he should be considered able" etc. |
| In kind | Out relief was given either in money or "in kind", loaves of bread, meat etc. |
| In-maintenance | The cost of maintaining a pauper in the workhouse. |
| Irremoveable | The pauper cannot be removed. See Acts of Parliament for explanation. |
| Medical Officer | See introduction. |
| Non-Resident Paupers | Paupers who belong to the Union but are residing within the area covered by a different Union. Their relief was paid, by arrangement, by the Union in which they resided. |
| Non-Settled Paupers | Paupers who resided within the area covered by the Union but belonged to a different Union. Their relief was paid, by arrangement, by the Union in which they resided. |
| Order for the House | Paupers were given a signed document addressed to the Workhouse Master ordering him to admit the pauper. |
| Out relief | Relief given outside the workhouse. In other than exceptional circumstances, out relief could only be given to a pauper who could produce a medical certificate or whose name, parish and complaint had been entered in the Medical Officer's book. |
| Overseer | See introduction. |
| Pensioner | Usually refers to an Army or Navy pensioner i.e. a Chelsea Pensioner or a Greenwich Pensioner. Pensioners who were in the workhouse usually signed over their pension to the Guardians who collected it on their behalf and used the money to pay their maintenance whilst in the workhouse. |
| Recognise | See "acknowledge" above. This has the same meaning. |
| Relieving Officer | See introduction. |

# GLOSSARY

| | |
|---|---|
| Removal order | If a pauper became chargeable to a parish, that parish could remove him to his place of settlement by an order of removal. The parish to which he was removed had 21 days to appeal against the order. |
| Suspended order | A removal order could be suspended if the pauper was too ill to be removed at the time. When the pauper was well again he could be sent on his way. The costs of his maintenance whilst the order was suspended would be claimed back from the parish to which he was removed. |
| To be sworn | The pauper is to be taken before a magistrate to give evidence as to his legal settlement or, in some cases, to be taken before a magistrate to give evidence as to the father of her child. |
| Union | e.g. "she resides in this Union" - the pauper resides in one of the parishes that comprise that particular Poor Law Union. |
| Vestry | A meeting of parishioners, or a group elected from the parishioners that met to discuss parish issues including poor law relief. |

# SOME ACTS OF PARLIAMENT RELATING TO POOR LAW

Many Acts of Parliament were passed that affected the Poor Law from 1834 onwards. The following has been extracted from a selection of these Acts, some very long, and it is hoped that these details will assist in interpreting the workhouse minutes.

**14 August 1834 (4 & 5 Wm IV).** *This is the very long Act that introduced the workhouses. The following is a very short précis of some of the articles*: Administration of relief to the poor is subject to the control of the Poor Law Commissioners. The giving of relief to the poor is under the control of the guardians or select vestry. Overseers may give temporary relief, in kind but not money, in cases of sudden and urgent necessity. Guardians may apply to the Quarter Sessions for bastardy orders. Paupers may be assisted to emigrate by the poor rate collected in their parish of settlement. From the passing of the act no settlement can be gained by hiring and service or by holding a parish office. Dangerous lunatics, insane persons and idiots must not be detained in workhouses for longer than 14 days. Employers of paupers who, having been given relief as loans have not repaid them, may extract a weekly sum from their wages to repay the loan. Husbands must maintain children, either legitimate or illegitimate, born to their wives before marriage. A pauper's parish of settlement is to bear the cost of his relief.

**17 August 1836 (6 & 7 Wm IV).** Civil Registration: the guardians are to create registrars' districts, appoint a Registrar of Births, Marriages and Deaths for each district, and provide a Register Office. The Clerk to the guardians, if qualified, may be appointed Superintendent Registrar for that Registration District. The Clerk to the guardians is to read notices of marriage that are not taking place by Licence, Special Licence or Banns, at three consecutive meetings of the Board of Guardians, and to keep Marriage Notice Books. If no objection is made to the marriage he may then issue a certificate so that the marriage can take place.

**26 August 1839 (2 & 3 Vic).** Provided that no application has been made to any Court of General Quarter Sessions, where bastards born since the 1834 Act are chargeable to any parish, the guardians of the parish or of the Union in which the parish is situated may apply, within three calendar months of the child becoming chargeable, to the Justices of the Peace holding any Petty Sessions Court for the division in which the Union is situated, for an order on the putative father to reimburse the Union or parish for its maintenance and support.

**23 July 1840 (3 & 4 Vic).** Vaccination: guardians of every parish are to contract with the medical officers of their Union for the vaccination of all persons resident in their Union or parish.

**10 August 1840 (3 & 4 Vic).** 1841 Census: every Registrar's district in England is to be formed into one or more enumeration districts. The Superintendent Registrar (usually the Clerk to the Board of Guardians) is to appoint enumerators.

**30 July 1842 (5 & 6 Vic).** Guardians are empowered to prescribe suitable employment for inmates, according to their capabilities, in return for food and lodging. Any pauper refusing or wilfully damaging the property of the guardians, including clothing is to be deemed and idle and disorderly person under the vagrancy laws. Lunacy: an annual list of lunatics is to be sent to the Clerk of the Peace for the county within which the parish to which the insane person is chargeable is situated, and to the Poor Law Commissioners.

**9 August 1844 (7 & 8 Vic).** Bastardy: the mother of a bastard child may make application to a Justice of the Peace at the Petty Sessions Court acting for the place where she resides for a summons to be served on the putative father. The evidence of the mother has to be corroborated. If an order is granted on the father is to pay a sum not exceeding 2s 6d per week until the child is 13 years of age. An annual return of orders and summonses is to be sent to the Clerk of the Peace who should send copies to the Home Secretary. Apprenticeship: guardians are to apprentice poor children instead of overseers of the poor, and the consent of a Justice of the Peace is not necessary. Relief: women whose husbands are overseas, in prison or in an asylum are to be treated as widows for the purposes of relief. Lunacy: expenses incurred for insane paupers may be levied off their estates.

**1846 (9 & 10 Vic).** Removal of the Poor: no person is to be removed from any parish in which he or she has resided for five years without serving in the army or navy, in prison, in an asylum, or having received relief during that time. Widows are not to be removed for twelve months after the death of their husbands. No child under 16, or sick paupers are to be removed except where the sickness or accident will produce permanent disability. [*These paupers are termed "irremoveable" in the minutes*]. Exemptions mentioned above do not qualify paupers to gain settlements in their place of residence.

**23 July 1847 (10 & 11 Vic).** Married inmates over 60 are not to be separated. Relief given to "irremoveable" paupers (see 9 & 10 Vic) to be charged to the General or Common Fund of the Union.

**4 September 1848 (11 & 12 Vic).** From the 30th September the cost of relief to wandering poor and foundlings, and their burials, are to be charged to the Common Fund. Relief given to paupers because of accident or sudden illness, who have a fixed place of abode with the Union but no legal settlement, should be charged to their place of abode, unless they are chargeable to the Common Fund. Emigration: guardians may assist any irremoveable pauper (chargeable to the General Fund) to emigrate [*to the British Colonies only*].

**1 August 1849 (12 & 13 Vic).** Guardians may appropriate money or possessions of paupers to repay the previous twelve months maintenance, and may reimburse themselves of the cost of burial in the same manner.

Another important event was the opening, in 1852, of the Pauper Lunatic Asylum at Bracebridge. At this time most of the Lincolnshire Unions transferred their lunatics to this new institution.